Never Endi

Third Edition

Reformed criminal turned criminologist, David Honeywell, shares his life story

David Honeywell

To Claire

Best Wishes

Dave

First published 2012 by Nocton Publishing
Second Edition 2014 and Third Edition 2015 by Beehive Books

ISBN: 978-0-9572599-6-6

A catalogue record for this book is available from the British Library

Cover design by Book Printing UK, Woodston, Peterborough
Printed and bound by Book Printing UK, Woodston, Peterborough

The publisher has used its best endeavours to ensure that the URLs for external websites referred to in this book are correct and active at the time of going to press. However, the publisher has no responsibility for the websites and can make no guarantee that a site with remain live or that the content is or will remain appropriate.

Every effort has been made to trace all copyright holders, but if any have been inadvertently overlooked the publisher will be pleased to include any necessary credits in any subsequent reprint or edition.

Contents

Acknowledgments

To my friends and family who have supported me throughout my troubled life and my decision to share my story. A big thank you to my mother, who is my best friend and has never stopped supporting me throughout everything. And also to my sister, Carol, who has always been there for me from when we were growing up together to this very day.

Always close to my heart is my late Uncle Donald, who encouraged me to study and use the pen rather than the sword. Had it not been for his influence, I doubt I would have ever entered university. Finally, I would like to thanks all those who have knowingly and unknowingly helped me turn my life around.

David Honeywell

November 2015

Publisher's Note

The author has changed the names of various people in the story that follows and it is not intended that any such individuals should be recognised, criticised or otherwise referred to in a personal or real life capacity. *Never Ending Circles* aims to offer encouragement to others who have had similar experiences and now wish to turn their lives around. And that David's story of crime, carrying knives and alcohol abuse, will help deter some young people from falling into the same life of self- destruction as he did, which ruins so many lives, he says.

It has three main objectives in mind. Firstly, because ordinary people can relate to ordinary people's lives, David hopes it will go some way towards helping others who may also suffer from mental health issues as he did.

Secondly, it can show young people how much crime can ruin their lives, by showing them the lifetime of struggles and torment he has had to endure as a result of his thoughtless actions which started as a youth. Thirdly, it is aimed at students and practitioners of criminology and related disciplines to use as a textbook to further their understanding of a person's criminal and anti-social behaviour and subsequent desistance from crime.

Introduction

Since publishing the first and second editions of Never Ending Circles, my life has changed dramatically and I'm pleased to say, for the better. When I published the first edition, I saw it as a finale to my life's journey but little did I know that it was merely the beginning of the next stage. At the time of writing this, I am enjoying teaching first year undergraduate students 'Crime and Deviance' at the University of York, where I am also working towards a PhD on the experiences of ex-prisoners who have entered higher education in relation to changing identities. I am also teaching as a part-time lecturer at Leeds Beckett University. I tour the country giving guest talks about my experiences and I am enjoying being part of the academic culture which embraced me from the day I was released from prison back in 1998. It seems that I lost the way for a while but my only crime during this time was to believe anyone other than the academic culture would give me a break in life.

Since graduating in 2003 with a Master's degree in Social Research Methods, I did little in the way of academic work. I attempted many different career paths, as this book explains, but prejudice and lack of opportunities held me back. It wasn't until 2012 that my passion for criminology resurfaced; mainly due to the interest I had received from the first edition of my book and my guest talks.

I have talked frankly and openly about my life journey, of my time in and out of institutions; about why I was incapable of holding down employment for many years; forming lasting relationships and how I developed an alcohol addiction. I also recount the many years I suffered with depression which plagued me from the tender age of 15. I was inspired to write this book after the riots broke out across

Britain in August 2011. In the wake of this devastation, many heated debates arose and questions were raised about disaffected youth, the lack of parental control in today's society, dysfunctional families, a breakdown in penal reform, zero crime deterrents, gang culture, and a need for strong role models within communities.

All of these things rang alarm bells with me so I decided to pen my own experiences in a bid to help others and put to rest many of my own demons. It's been a humbling experience to write my story, some of it daunting, some of it poignant and some of it funny.

It has brought back many forgotten memories both good and bad. It has also been a personal learning experience in itself. I have been pleasantly surprised at the general response from the public which has been nothing but positive. I have learned a lot more about myself and it has even reunited me with many of those from my past I had lost contact with over the years.

If I could turn the clock back, I most definitely would, but as I can't, I can at least try to help others. I was aged 20 before I got my first criminal convictions for two attempted robberies resulting in a 30 month youth custody sentence. I then spent the rest of my early adult years drifting through different towns and cities and had too many jobs to remember. I also committed relatively petty, mostly impulsive, but occasionally violent crimes such as criminal damage and common assault. My directionless way of life also included several periods in psychiatric hospitals for clinical depression. Then in July 1995, I was given a five year prison sentence for 'wounding with intent to cause grievous bodily harm'. I went to prison, an un-educated individual with massive failings to overcome but with a new determination to turn things around. Seven years after leaving prison, I graduated with a bachelor's degree in criminology followed two years later with a Master's degree in Social Research Methods.

After my Master's degree in 2003, I attempted to build a career in Journalism, starting with writing for the university's student newspaper. Then in 2005, my first article for a regional newspaper appeared in the *York Press* (now called, *The Press*) and for several years to come, I had many articles published and earned a living writing press releases . It eventually fizzled out though as I realised that I was going nowhere. But it seems things are meant to happen and now as the second half of my life begins, I am looking towards a bright future with a new career as an academic and exciting opportunities.

1. Where it all began

I was born on 1st August 1963 on a Royal Air Force base called *Nocton Hall* in Lincolnshire to Eric and Nancy Honeywell. I also have one sister, Carol, who is five years older than me. My father was originally from Eston near Middlesbrough and my mother was from Fulford in York. Because my father was serving in the Royal Air Force, we moved around a lot from one camp to another every two or three years.

As a result of this, our schooling became quite disrupted and our lives became quite unsettled, because as soon as we'd made friends, we were on the move again. Every school had a different system, teaching methods, curriculums and routines. I also seem to recall that some teachers had the attitude that because we wouldn't be there for very long anyway, there wasn't a lot of point investing too much time in us.

There was also a very different attitude from certain teachers towards the kids from camp compared to the local kids who the teachers had seen through infants and primary and whose parents they had forged friendships with over the years.

I can remember these very early feelings of isolation and prejudice. We were outcasts wherever we went but there were lots of other children of RAF parents in our position. Some of them had been living abroad for several years and then had to suddenly readjust to life in Britain. From when I was three, we lived for about five years on a middle class housing estate called Summerfield Drive in Porthcawl, South Wales. My father was stationed at the nearby RAF, St Athan. Porthcawl holds wonderful memories for me during this period of my early childhood in the 1960's - a time I often reminisce with my mother. I can recall my mother showing me what Hippies and Beatniks were and I remember those flowered coloured

Beetle cars they used to drive around in. It was the first time I was introduced to prejudice too. There were a lot Welsh natives who didn't much like the English, but this was just the beginning of a lifetime of bigotry for me. The RAF used to organise massive family events such as *Battle of Britain* displays every September where all the families could go and enjoy a gala day. We would see the *Red Arrows*, the RAF gymnastics squad and dog handler displays. We also got chance to sit inside aeroplanes to have our photographs taken, then there would be the usual stalls and games. At Christmas time, they used to organise magnificent parties for all the kids. We all spent the first part of the day watching cartoons at the cinema followed by a tea party in a huge hall which had a large Christmas tree and a stack of presents in one corner for all the kids.

Santa would enter the hall on a sleigh and then each child's name was individually called out for them to go and collect their presents. Not far from us, was a local amusement park in Porthcawl called Coney Beach with all the rides and excitement fayres can bring. From our house, you could hear the crowds and screams from people on the rollercoaster rides and you could see flashing lights everywhere. In 1971, we left Wales and moved to RAF Hullavington (now Buckley Barracks), near Chippenham, Wiltshire. When you are moved on to another base in the military, it is referred to as being 'posted'. We lived in a four-bedroom house known as a 'married quarter'. Married quarters are houses provided for military personnel and their families to live in. When we lived in these houses, there were certain archaic rules laid down by the RAF for families to adhere to. For example, all the families on camp had to use their regulation furniture and if you marked or damaged anything, you would be charged for it. We could not have wallpaper; we had to use their regimental green or blue paint on the walls. My father was always getting on to Carol and I, reminding us not to mark the walls or furniture. Every time we moved house, two officials from the Department of Environment (DOE) would pay us a visit to conduct a thorough inspection. They would run their fingers along the door frames and shelves, checking for dust and inspect for marks on the walls. I can clearly see them now slowly reading down their endless check list examining everything in sight, from cutlery and crockery, to walls, floors and even the back garden.

On one occasion, we were all sat in the car ready to set off to our new home when the inspectors ordered my father go back into the garden with a shovel and break the soil he had turned over earlier, into smaller chunks because they felt that they were too big.

My mother told me recently that on the day of these moves while waiting for the inspectors to turn up, she was constantly on edge with two kids running around, worrying, in case we marked the walls or furniture. She was even too scared to cook our dinner in case she marked the cooker. Everything in the house was grey, blue or green, including the walls and carpets. The upside for kids though, was that we got to see a lot of aeroplanes and activity as we lived so close to the airfields and runways. This was also a great place for us to ride our bikes in the vast, free, empty space. You had to always keep a look out for the red warning lights at the gates though as the Parachute Regiment used to train there. You would see soldiers, large trucks and hardware descending from *Hercules* aircraft.

When the red lights were on, you stayed off the runways. If by chance, you happened to get caught halfway across when they lit up, the 'Snowdrops' (RAF police), would be there in minutes to escort you away in a *Land Rover*.

In 1973, we moved to RAF Leeming in North Yorkshire and it was here that my life would start to change for the worse. I was ten years old and although I always kept a few select friends, I spent a lot of time in my bedroom playing records on an old fashioned record player that had seen better days.

The Bay City Rollers were all the rage then and all my friends were wearing the latest tartan clad trousers and tops with baseball boots. Whenever I asked my father if he would buy me some clothes so I could look the same as the other kids, as always, I was abruptly refused.   This was usual for him. I remember, once having to beg him for a new pair of shoes because the ones I was wearing had holes in the bottoms and my socks would get soaked on wet days. Families who lived on RAF camps were a mixture of all different classes. I use the term 'class' because the military always made sure people knew *exactly* which class they belonged to. Lower ranks and commissioned officers' families were separated into different communities on the camp. There was a real snobbery in the forces, which I later came across during my own stint in the army. Whenever there was a formal dance or a ball, the notice board would display an invitation which would read something along the lines of, 'Officers will bring their ladies - Warrant officers and senior ranks will bring their wives - NCOs (non-commissioned officers), will bring their women.'

The definition of an NCO is an enlisted member of the armed forces, such as a corporal, Sergeant, or petty officer, appointed to a rank conferring leadership over other enlisted personnel.

Not only was this sheer snobbery, but totally untrue in many cases because some of the officer's wives were anything but ladies. My mother used to clean houses for some of them and she would tell me that a lot of the officer's wives wore their husband's rank, thinking that they were a cut above the rest. In fact, most were very ordinary people looking down their noses at everyone else. Yet, the higher in rank the officers were, the more genuine and 'down to earth' they and their wives seemed to be. As always, the 'jumped up' were the worst.

My grandmother, who was an army wife used to tell my mother exactly the same. I saw a real class divide on these camps and it was here that I learned to despise some of the upper echelons of society and see them for what they really were.

I can remember when I was in the army, one of the squaddies was dating a Major's daughter. One sunny Saturday afternoon they invited me and a friend along with them to her home. I instantly saw the disapproval on her mother's patronising face as she looked down her nose at us from across their very plush living room. She then asked her daughter if she could have a word in private. I knew what was coming next because I had seen it all before. Low and behold my friend and I were then asked to leave by the embarrassed young daughter. It seemed hypocritical that although her daughter was allowed to date an army Private, a select few army buddies were unwelcome at her home. Living in the military as a child had already opened my eyes to the unbearable snobbery amongst the ranks.

The earliest years in South Wales were by far the happiest for me as I remember, but I still look back with fond memories of not only Wales, but also RAF, Hullavington and Leeming. Nevertheless, at the time, I was too young to see that underneath the surface, things were not so happy at home.

My mother didn't have a very happy life with my father. Apart from being generally ill-tempered, he would often lash out at her for the slightest thing. She'd get the occasional black eye or bleeding nose which she and Carol would always try to hide from me by pretending she'd had an accident. I got a pair of boxing gloves for Christmas one year. The next day I saw my mother with a black eye; she told me that she and my father had been larking around with my boxing gloves and he had accidently hit her too hard. I learned the truth years later.

My father was also extremely greedy and tight with money. After bed-time, Carol and I would sometimes hear them shouting at each other downstairs and we would lie in our beds listening, scared stiff and wondering what might happen next.

2. Playground Bullies

It was during my secondary school years in the 1970's when I first saw someone get a good kicking from a gang. It was actually on my behalf too. The gang leader, Tabby Taylor, who liked my sister, had heard that a third year had attacked me. I had accidently snapped a small pendant he had made in metal work class so he head butted me. I watched by as Tabby Taylor and his gang of about seven, chased him into the boy's changing rooms and laid into him. I was never interested in being part of a gang but seeing him get his just deserts gave me a real sense of satisfaction.

My youth was plagued by bullies who destroyed any self-esteem or confidence I'd ever had, which wasn't much anyway - thanks to my father. I know many people go through this during their school years, but while some seem to get over it, others are scarred for life and of course, some kids are bullied far worse than others.

I was an easy target. I had a mop of bright ginger hair, as well as being very shy and timid. I wouldn't say 'boo to a goose' and it wasn't helped by the fact that I stood out like a 'sore thumb'. Not being dressed in the fashion of the day like the other kids, did little for my self confidence and made it impossible for me to blend in. I also wore other peoples' cast offs and all because my father was so tight with money. My father basically set us up for a life of misery at the hands of bullies.

One of the most important lessons I learned in life about bullies though, (which would hold me in good stead for the future), was how cowardly they really are and how you should always stand up to them. It was after my transition from primary to secondary school at the age of 11, when bullies started to target me most of all. I started attending Bedale Secondary School in North Yorkshire when we lived at RAF Leeming. Although I've endured many other hardships in my adult life, my teenage school years were some of the most traumatic of all; I was powerless. Most of what happened to me later in life was of my own doing, but during my childhood years I was an innocent victim of bullies. I couldn't even escape them after the school bell had gone because some were also my neighbours.

Overnight, I changed from being a happy child into a withdrawn, depressed, nervous wreck because of bullying and the school's failure to do anything about it. One day, I begged my father to let me stay off school as I couldn't take the bullying anymore. I remember him walking me to school and as we got closer, I was pleading with him to not make me stay. He insisted on seeing the headmaster, Mr Ramsay, with me present. Mr Ramsay persuaded me to report the culprits, after which my life became hell.

I must have looked so unhappy back then because at school one day, a lady teacher passing me on the stairs suddenly stopped me and with a concerned expression on her face and said, "Oh cheer up, why do you look so sad?"

I really wanted to offload everything to her, but I had already learned the consequences of speaking out. I felt that the only way to stay safe was to bottle things up. She was one of the nicer teachers, but for many years, I blamed teachers for failing to protect me and other bullied kids like myself. The ringleaders at Bedale School were two real losers and as always, with bullies, they were very different on their own.

One was a large kid, who thought he was a tough nut because of his oversized body. He fancied himself as a football hooligan too. One day, when he was taunting me in the school woodwork class, poking me in the face, I just snapped and let rip with a real good right hand punch to his nose making it bleed. My father had been showing me the night before how I should punch him the next time he picked on me. This was a turning point for me as I now realised that I was capable of standing up to bullies. I felt a sort of new confidence grow inside me after that. The taunting never went away altogether, but I always knew that when push came to shove, I could hurt someone. Most importantly, they now knew that too. It also made me aware how cowardly bullies really are. Being bullied taught me to detect weakness in bullies and from that day on, whenever someone pushed me too far, I lashed out.

It was difficult to concentrate on studying with all this going on, but my favourite subjects were Art, Music and English Language. I was always able to write well from a very young age. I know full well, that had it not been for such a tormented school life, I would have excelled in my studies. One of my teachers told my parents (as all my school reports stated) that I was above average intelligence, but lacked concentration. Well, what did they expect?

I also hated PT (physical training) classes or Games as they were called in one school, because I wasn't good at it. The bigger, tougher kids always brow beat the weaker ones and while the confident pupils demonstrated their sporting talents, the less confident ones were humiliated.

I would purposely leave my PT kit at home, even though I knew I would get slippered for it. I was so nervous and self conscious about my lack of sporting skills. In 1976, my father had completed his 22 years military service, so we then moved to his home town of Middlesbrough.

We lived at 12 Monmouth Road, Eston. Some would say it's nearer Grangetown and some would say Eston, but it's always been Grangetown to me. My new school was Sarah Metcalfe Secondary. Though I was bullied at Bedale School, Sarah Metcalfe was a much rougher school. The school today, (now called Eston Park) is nothing like its former self when I was there. It is situated on a large recreation field known as 'the rec' and at the time it was close to three other schools.

There were often running battles between each school and a constant rivalry. After my second day at Sarah Metcalfe, while on my way home with a new school friend, I was jumped by a gang of about six pupils from one of the other schools. I was head butted and punched to the ground, then repeatedly kicked in the face. One thing that always sticks in my mind was the terrified expression on my friends face looking back at me as he ran like hell. A woman was hammering on her living room window as the kicks kept coming. I was a mess and lost a tooth, but most of all I was affected psychologically and emotionally. The next day, Carol, who was always a rock whenever I needed her help, took me to their school in search of justice. We were then taken to a classroom where I recognised them instantly and without a care in the world, I pointed each one of them out. I can't remember how we managed to find the right class. Perhaps it was my description that rang a bell with the headmaster before we went looking for them.

My father, didn't react whatsoever when he saw my cuts and bruises. He had been working that day and when he came home, I was shocked by his lack of caring. School was a soul destroying place. Sarah Metcalfe had the reputation of enlisting some of the poorest kids from the most disadvantaged pockets of society. Here, I witnessed the dreaded 'class divide' all over again. It seemed we were looked down on by the nearby former grammar school, Gillbrook, and other more select schools. Those that had the confidence to excel, were given the utmost encouragement and praise by teachers, while the lesser achievers were practically 'written-off'.

I didn't go back to school for most of my fifth year; I gave up on education. The school had let me down, my father had let me down and I was just not interested in any of the subjects they taught anyway.

I could not believe that something like Religious Education could be compulsory; I hated most subjects except for those I've mentioned. However, I had to start attending school again for the latter part of my fifth year after being warned by my teachers. Then, one day, only about five of us turned up for PT classes because most the others were away on a school trip to Hexham. The PT teacher took us all over to Eston recreation ground 'the rec' and had us run laps around it. For the first time ever, I excelled. I had found a sport that I was a natural at and I was even encouraged by the teacher for once, who shouted, "Go on, Honeywell! You'll be a champ one day!" Although I know this was a 'tongue in cheek' remark, it was enough to change me. It boosted my self-confidence enormously and from that day onwards, I have continued to run. I also started weight training and joining in other fitness activities at the local sports hall which, until then, I had always avoided at all costs. Another reason that I was spurned on to start using weights was because one day, I took a severe beating from a bigger kid, who was a regular gym user. He actually later became my first ever training partner.

The academic side of things was not so good; my deviant behaviour had begun to emerge now; I had started to steal from my mother. One day, I was summoned to the headmaster's office after she had visited the school that day asking for help as she struggled to raise an unruly, adolescent boy on her own. Her once angelic little boy was turning into a thief. Mr Smith stormed into the classroom and in front of the entire class, bellowed, "Honeywell! In my office now!"

The class started to snigger and make remarks as I followed Mr Smith obediently, embarrassed by all the attention. His office was a tiny box room situated not far from my classroom. It had a fusty smell with old books scattered around. My biology teacher, Mr Belmont was there too. Nose to nose, Belmont began screaming in my face as Smith sat in his chair looking on. I was trembling, with feelings of anxiety soaring through my entire body. I was being judged as some kind of reprobate, crying and shaking, as he screamed:

"Do you love your mother!?"
"Yes!" I said, trying to control my quivering bottom lip.
"And yet you would do a dirty trick like this to her?"

I began to cry and could see the sudden realisation on their faces that they had done their job. Pity they hadn't done this to my bullies, then perhaps I wouldn't have felt the need to steal money to keep them from beating me up. I knew that what I had done was wrong, but as with all my teachers, they had failed to see the bigger picture. During exam week, I walked into the school hall, where other pupils were taking their places at the rows of tables, but instead of joining them, I looked on with a sinking feeling, thinking to myself, 'what's the point?'. I turned around, left, and never returned. At least, not until 30 years later, when in 2009, I was invited to present badges at the Annual Prefect Ceremony. This was one of the major turning points in my life. My former music teacher was now the Assistant Head, and nearing retirement. I had always dreamt of going back to school as an adult one day to put my inner demons to rest. I had contacted Mr Hall about possibly visiting and he saw an opportunity for his former pupil-turned-publicist to celebrate the school's history by chronicling its past and present. I interviewed teachers and former pupil, now famous actor, Mark Benton as part of it. I had seen him many times on my television screen but had never met him, even though we were at the same school at the same time. The whole experience was surreal.

Since my school days, I have since embraced education and the teachers who I had always held responsible for my failings and for not helping me when I was being bullied as a young boy, were now my peers. I left school an uneducated, angry young man and returned a Master of Science and entrepreneur.

I would not have passed a single exam back in '79 anyway, because I had been playing truant for most of that year. Unbelievably though, ever since that day when we were made to run around the recreation ground, my then most feared subject, which was PT would now become a way of life for me.

Two years later, when I joined the army. I was super-fit and one of the most confident soldiers in the gym. I confidently climbed the ropes, was able to clear the wooden horse, climb the wall frames and stay ahead of all the others on every single platoon run. I achieved the highest ever fitness score on record at Blackdown Barracks in Deepcut, Surrey during basic training and years later, I fulfilled a lifelong ambition to become a qualified fitness instructor. What a difference one teacher's remark can make to a child's self-esteem.

3. Family Blues

After we moved to Middlesbrough, tension had now started to build at home as my father struggled to adapt to civilian life. He became even more unpredictable and struggled to hold down a job. Then, not long after, Carol and I were both hit with a bombshell! My parents sat us both down one evening and announced they were getting divorced. I remember Carol bursting into tears and I just sat there stunned. I didn't cry because I was always taught, 'boys don't cry'. Things had been going downhill for a while since my dad left the forces as he struggled to settle, but there had been problems for many years. The only reason my parents had stayed together for as long as they did, was because my mother did not want us my sister and I to suffer a family break up. There were many occasions she could have just left my father and had it not been for the RAF persuading her not to divorce him years earlier, this would have happened a long time sooner.

I remember as a child, always being terrified of my mother leaving us. I was always begging her not to run away. I know sometimes when she had a row with my dad, she would wander off for hours just to get some space. I developed huge insecurities over this; thinking she would never come back. Although I knew my parents had their fair share of problems over the years, the break up was still a huge shock to us. The worst part for me, was being made to choose which parent I wanted to stay with. Given that my mother was the good parent, my choice was obvious, but my father, wanting to see my mother out on the streets, bullied me into verbally choosing who I wanted to stay with. One day, he took me to see my grandmother, who didn't live far away. On the way back, he suddenly pulled the car over to the side of the road. He looked at me and said, "You have to choose which one of us you want to stay with now!

I felt tormented and confused. One day, he followed me in to my bedroom, demanding I make this decision once and for all. My mother joined us and pleaded with him to stop pressurising me. He punched her in the side of her neck, knocking her onto my bed. If there had been any doubt in my mind who I wanted to stay with, after that moment, I had no doubt whatsoever.

I blurted out, "I'm staying with my mother! Why did you have to do that?"

With a smile on his face, my father replied, "It was a good right-hander though wasn't it, Dave?"

I rushed outside to my sister's house; she was now living only three doors away. I hammered on her door but she was out. I ran to the telephone box at the other end of the street, when I saw a police officer leaving someone's house.

My mother had caught up with me by now. She was crying.

"Can you please help us?" I asked, "My father has just punched my mother."

"We can't get involved, I'm afraid," said the officer. "It's a domestic and we can't interfere."

From that day on, I knew that the only way to deal with bullies was to take the law into my own hands.

My father treated me like dirt after that night. One evening, we were both sat in the living room watching television, he was now giving me permanent silent treatment. I had been to the dentist that day to have some teeth extracted and was feeling unwell from the effects of the gas. I suddenly spewed up all over the living room floor.

He just sat there without saying a single word and watched me scrub my vomit up. When my father was in a bad mood, he used to always take it out on us. Sometimes, he would stop speaking for days at a time if he'd had a row with my mother. He would not only stop speaking to my mother for days on end though, but us kids too, the innocent victims caught up in it all. The atmosphere was horrendous; you could cut it with a knife. For days and days, we had to walk on eggshells, scared stiff of upsetting him in case we got the backlash. I left that year and grew up with a particular hatred towards men who bullied or were violent towards women and children. The months following my parents' divorce in 1978, were the worst of our lives and that summer I was admitted into St Luke's Psychiatric Hospital (Adolescent Unit) in Middlesbrough.

Even today, I cannot tolerate long silences. If I am in a room with other people, I have to speak or get them to speak. If I ever have an argument with a girlfriend, I can't take the silent treatment, I have to clear the air. I will always try to make up if that is what it takes, but if I feel it has come to the point where we can no longer communicate, then it is time to move on. It was a particularly unhappy time of my life and choosing a parent was something I never dreamed I would ever have to do. Carol didn't need to do this as she was nineteen at the time, whereas I being only fourteen, was still a minor. She was going out with a nice lad called Gerald (Ged), who lived only a few doors away, so she was able to escape it to a point.

I know the whole ordeal had a devastating effect on her emotionally though. Ged saw her washing my father's car one day, and asked her out on a date. It was a fairytale romance and they've been happily married now for over 30 years.

They have two lovely daughters, my nieces, and I am proud to say that recently, I became a Great Uncle. I always sort of envied my sister's life. That sort of happiness is all I have ever wanted and I could never understand why I could not have the same. The family break up was messy, with lots of arguments and interference from in-laws and it was around this time that my deviant behaviour started to emerge. I was around the age of 15. It started with me playing truant from school. Quite often, I get asked when it all started to change for me. Well, this was it! As I emotionally struggled to deal with the breakup of my parents, practically overnight, a drastic change in my behaviour started to surface.

It was not just the fact that they were separating, but it was the way my father dealt with the situation and how his family caused so much trouble over it despite it having absolutely nothing to do with them. As well as truancy, there were several other wayward things I started to do that were out of character. I began stealing, flying into rages, refusing to conform, rebelling against authority and shutting myself off from the outside world. It was a strange time. My dad continued living under the same roof as us for a while due to an agreement whereby he and my mother had to live separate lives but in the same house. This was just soul destroying for the rest of us.

He even had his own separate food cupboard with a padlock attached to it to stop us from stealing any of his food. Sometimes he forgot to lock it, so I stole what I could. Before my parents had announced their impending divorce, I had been what you may have described as a model child.

I spent most of my early teenage years locking myself in my bedroom. My bedroom became my first prison. It was a place where I could shut myself away for hours a day to avoid the world. I did not need anyone else. I became such a recluse and started acting oddly - becoming even more withdrawn, not speaking, barely leaving the house and now, totally incapable of socialising.

It was also a time when it was not the 'norm' to be from a broken home - so I felt even more isolated. It was from this point, I began to get labelled by others. Coming from a broken home in the 1970's was taboo. I couldn't talk to anyone about it and I didn't know anyone else who had divorced parents. I started to become angry and very bitter.

My mother was now left to fend for herself where previously, she had my father's income, albeit a pittance and an insult. Because of the lack of money available, she used to make some of our clothes, knit, darn and mend. She made do with what she had as she could afford very little. Carol and I got 50 pence a week pocket money in return for household chores.

During the height of the divorce proceedings, Social Services had started to get involved. They felt, that with the strain of my father still living under the same roof as us and the stress of the divorce, that my mother and I should have a short break away somewhere. They took us to a remote farm in Barnard Castle, County Durham, where we were to live for a week in an old converted barn. The barn was a cold, stone building just inside the farm gates, with steps leading up to it. Inside, was a shabby settee and chair in one room and a bunk bed in the other.

At night, you could hear the mice or rats scratching away. There were cobwebs everywhere and yet somehow, we managed to make the best of it. One of the ladies from Social Services handed my mother four pounds for the week for us both to live on. Day by day, my mother meticulously planned out what we could eat and how much we could spend. After all, she'd had plenty of practice over the years living on the small amounts of money she'd had to beg from my father.

The money soon ran out, so my mother decided it was time to head home a few days earlier than planned.

Eventually, my father left us to go and live on his own while seeing his new woman he'd met at work. He worked at the local sports hall in Eston as a caretaker, where I used to train in the gym.

It didn't bother him how it might be making me feel, seeing him flirting with her. It was heartbreaking to think that while my mother was sat at home suffering the consequences of the break up, he blatantly courted his new lady friend right under my nose. My mother is the most loyal person I know and in many ways, too good for this world. She never met anyone else after my father.

4. In Need of a Role Model

The transformation that started to take place in me around this time was significant because I was going through puberty and desperate for a strong male role model in my life. I was taking more of an interest in girls, whereas at school I was just a 'drop-out' kid. Now, with all the weight training and exercise I was doing, I was starting to develop a good physique and athletic prowess. My father had left home by now, but had never been a role model anyway. There was only myself and my mother at home, so who could I speak to about girls or the changes going on inside me that I didn't understand?

I couldn't talk to my mother about 'man' things and we'd never talked about things in our family anyway. It had never been encouraged to discuss things of a sensitive nature such as girls or the 'birds and bees'. Everything was 'hush hush'. Inside of me was a desperate young lad with raging hormones desperate for guidance. We never saw any sign of affection at home and I found it difficult to display this later in life, until I started courting when it then became an outpouring of misguided emotion. It was quite suffocating for those I showered with affection.

My first love, who I met in York, couldn't get me to hold hands in public. It took her several weeks to get me to succumb to this, as I had never done it before. I know my unnatural upbringing of not seeing affection or being able to talk about things went a long way towards me developing a rather stunted and disturbed personality. My mother was always affectionate, but generally, things were not talked about or displayed. I just didn't know how to behave, I was either emotionally over the top or emotionless. This was the root cause of my oppressed social skills. When I was suffering, I didn't know how to communicate my feelings, nor did I have anyone to communicate them to. My problems and emotions then festered away inside me for many years to come. Carol had moved in with Ged by now and I felt even more isolated. I know my mother had great concerns about my behaviour too. I was starting to become more and more disobedient and erratic, taking advantage of the fact that there was no dominant male around to control me. She carried on trying to stay strong and keep me on the right track while at the same time struggling with the divorce.

Around this time, my grandfather, Harry, (my father's father) felt it would be a good idea to get more involved with the family. He did help us a lot by offering advice and supporting my mother through it all. After all, he knew my father better than anyone and had despised the way he'd treated us. It was also clear that there was huge resentment between the two of them spanning many years.

My father's mother had never liked my mother and had always made it quite clear she wasn't welcome in the family. She'd always blamed her for taking her precious son away from her and just picked on her all the time. The truth was, he couldn't wait to escape her overbearing clutches. She also picked on my mother because she spoke and acted differently. She picked on her every word.

The kitchen at my grandmother's was the hub of gossip and secret whispers. You could walk in and it would go silent. It's where the world was 'put to rights' and all the malicious tongue-wagging took place. My grandfather, however, was a more placid type of person. We eventually decided that he should move into our family home as he could give us back some stability. Also, he was unhappy living with my grandmother who was one of the most vicious natured women I have ever met. We had a spare room and we all got on well, so he came to live with us. However, not long after, underlying problems began to surface.

For one, I would not be told what to do. I was 15 and I had just seen the back of a domineering, controlling father. My grandfather's mannerisms and personality traits were exactly the same as my fathers. This was like a red rag to a bull. It is a well-known fact that you don't really know a person until you live with them, and this was a perfect example. He would lecture me and try to brow beat my mother and I. My mother would, as always, defend me to the hilt, while trying to keep the peace at the same time. I could hear them always arguing about me.

I would sit at the bottom of the stairs on the other side of the door, listening to him criticising me, telling her how much of a bad son I was. I would listen to their every word, slowly going out of my mind. It was at this time of my life I started to develop paranoia, another significant change in my personality, which then led to violent outbursts. This often resulted in me shouting or smashing things to pieces in violent rages brought on by sheer frustration.

It was obvious that my mother had become dependent on my grandfather as he was now paying the bills and had a real hold over us. His overbearing manner and arrogance would just 'fuel the fire' and tear my life apart. My mother was torn, she needed all the support she could get - which my grandfather provided, yet she wanted her son to be happy too. I've always felt cheated having never experienced the support and care of loving grandparents. Apart from the tormented experience I had living with my grandfather, there was never any bond or affection from my grandmother either.

On my mother's side of the family, I have heard so many great things about her parents. My mother's father was a staff Sergeant in the Yorkshire Regiment and a survivor of the Somme. He had also fought in the Boer War and during the Second World War, he worked as an Air Raid Warden in York. He had been stationed in Germany then Catterick and Strensall barracks over his 30 year army career. An orphan with a horrific childhood, he had lied about his age to enlist into the army and in 1899 at the age of 15, went to fight in the second Boer War. Joining the army was his preferred choice to the alternative of being sent away to work as a servant.

My grandmother was born in Camden Town in London. She was a very talented pianist and a very proud woman. She was a religious, well read lady who came from a strict Victorian background. Sadly, they both died when I was only one-years-old, so I have no memories of them at all. Instead, I only have memories of the cold, shallow side of my father's grandparents. My mother was worried about how withdrawn and disturbed I'd become, so she suggested I went to see a child psychologist to which I agreed. We both went together to St Luke's Hospital in Middlesbrough. The psychologist agreed that my resentment towards my grandfather and his domineering presence in the house was extremely damaging and unsettling. It was mutually agreed that I should become an outpatient at their Adolescent Unit. Later, it was decided that I should be an inpatient, which I was for three months. This was a ward for disturbed teenagers from difficult backgrounds. It seemed bizarre to most adults that a 15 year old could suffer from depression. I learned very quickly that there was a lot of stigma and ignorance surrounding depression. It was very much misunderstood in those days and still is today. There was a very strict German nurse and a husband and wife team running the ward. I was given a job in the main stores which would lead to my first step on the career ladder.

Each day, I would walk from the adolescent unit across to the main stores, through all the corridors, where I would pass lots of adult patients on the way. When I was delivering supplies around the hospital wards with my workmate, who was also from the adolescent unit, I would see some very scary people.

From my child's eyes, I saw them as people who could potentially attack me at any moment. The very sight of some of them talking to themselves, the way they stared at me and their strange physical appearances, was terrifying. It was like walking amongst the living dead. Some looked just like zombies with them being spaced out on tranquillisers.

During one of my weekend home visits, I bought a guitar and was trying to teach myself some chords, when by chance, my mother met new neighbours, Dennis and Janet Shaw. They had three children and lived directly opposite us and had not long been in our street.

She later sent me over to introduce myself to Dennis, who was a brilliant guitarist and vocalist. He had spent many years touring the pubs and clubs. He was a resident singer at the Oak Leaf in South

Bank during his youth and a close friend of comedian Roy Chubby Brown. I immediately struck up a friendship and bond with the whole family. I became very attached to them as I was in desperate need of a family life and father figure. Each night, I went across to their house to escape the miserable atmosphere at home. Dennis taught me more chords each day and how to play until, eventually, I became quite competent.

At meal times, Janet would always include me with the family and it would sometimes be after 11pm before I returned home. My grandfather was always needling me that I was begging to be part of their family. It was true, but as I pointed out to him, it was only because of his son's and his own failure to be good role models.

Eventually, I actually moved in and lived with the Shaw family for quite a while. Dennis became the most important male role model to me during my teenage years. He took me under his wing calling me the 'son he'd never had'. He was a tough character, a weight lifting champion with a black belt in Judo and he was well respected in the community. His influence over me was paramount during my early development of masculinity. I took on the mantle by following his example and excelling in weight training and martial arts.

He was everything a young male needed in a role model. He had good morals and a strong work ethic. I idolised him and he helped me more than he probably ever realised. I know that he felt let down whenever I got into trouble and I felt I'd let him down too. There's no doubt that had it not been for Dennis toughening me up, I couldn't have survived army training and prison life the way I did. He did talk to me about the 'birds and the bees' and helped me pluck up the courage to ask a girl out on my first ever date. He explained things to me only a father and son could discuss. I let him down over and over again. Despite his endless patience, giving me good advice and trying to steer me in the right direction, the damage had already been done years before. He always said he wished he had got me when I was younger. Sadly, Dennis died in 2008 aged 65, but I will never forget how he helped me through my mixed-up adolescence. Writing his obituary for the local press was one of the hardest narratives I have ever written. I still grew up with massive failings to overcome and deep seated problems, but Dennis had given me the tools to survive. Most importantly though, I would one day find myself giving the same advice to other young men, as he had me. I had listened and I had learned. It was merely just a matter of time before I was strong enough to put it all into practice.

5. Bring back National Service!

Although my disastrous, and brief army career ended after only one year, I am adamant that I managed to draw some invaluable experiences from it. Although I was dishonourably discharged and later landed myself in prison, I had learned self-discipline, self-respect, as well as respect for authority, the importance of fitness and good manners. In the end, it was my choice to rebel against army rules and break the law, but this was no reflection on what I had learned from the army. I never forgot the positive things I was taught and I was always able to call on this discipline whenever I needed it.

Ironically, it made prison easier when I ended up there several years later, but at least I gleaned the most important elements of army life. It would do no harm to instil this into today's youth. National Service would teach the skills I learned. I admit I started to go off the rails once I started drinking alcohol and it was the army that introduced me to it, but my real problems were already deeply rooted.

I had officially left school in 1979 into a recession and with no qualifications or job prospects whatsoever. The North was hit hard with unemployment and I could see no future if I had stayed in Middlesbrough. The best solution, I felt was to join the forces, it would give me a trade and straighten me out - or so I thought. I was 16 at the time and had been working on the Youth Opportunities Programme (YOP) at the ICI Chemical Plant. This was a government scheme for helping 16 to 18 year olds into employment. I was paid £23.50 a week and was moved around the site every few weeks to gain different experiences, starting in the post room for a while, then at Wilton Golf Course, where I got chance to drive a tractor and help maintain the grounds. I was then sent to work in the main stores. The

YOP scheme was temporary, so I set my heart on joining the RAF. I think there was something about the forces life that I missed from my
childhood. I blew my YOP placement when I got caught stealing from work. One day, one of my co-workers saw me sneaking a box of pencils that I'd stolen from the stores into my locker and immediately reported me to the boss. We hadn't liked one another from day one. He had a real problem with me for some reason, so this was his way of getting one over on me. I was later called into the office and dismissed immediately. So many people believe that taking things from the workplace is acceptable, but it is in fact still a crime. It is theft after all and this was the beginning of my criminal behaviour, however much people may think it trivial.

I had an appointment at the RAF careers office and was really excited about the prospect of a career in the services, but my excitement was soon to be shattered. Already, my past was about to start spoiling things for me - something that would become a regular occurrence throughout the rest of my life.

My medical records showed I'd been in St Luke's Hospital for depression which immediately put obstacles in my way. I remember the recruitment officer at Borough Road in Middlesbrough telling me that I needed a doctor's note to state I was fit to join up. So I made the long bus journey to my doctor's surgery in Normanby to get the note that would give me a chance to start a new life. It would help me secure a career that would change my life forever. However, the doctor ruined any chance I had of this happening. I excitedly took the same long bus journey back to Middlesbrough with the doctor's note sealed inside an envelope. Once I was back at the careers office, I eagerly waited for the recruitment officer to read it and then tell me I could go ahead with enlisting.

My heart began to sink as I saw a puzzled expression come over his face as he read it to himself. To our surprise, the doctor had written that I was unfit to join. 'Thanks Doc,' I thought, 'Thanks for ruining the only chance of something positive happening in my life.'

I quickly learned that you can't let things keep you down for long though. You always need a 'plan B'. After the initial shock of being turned away, I tried to join several of the other armed services. I sat tests for the Merchant Navy and Royal Marines, but failed every one of them. Even if I had been given the chance of taking things further with the RAF, I would have failed the entrance test anyway.

I remember sitting the entrance exam for the Merchant Navy along with a few other hopefuls. Afterwards, we all sat waiting for our results. I glanced across at two of the examiners who I noticed were looking across at me while whispering to one another. I felt so sad because I knew that I'd failed.

My failed schooling was now starting to make my life a misery, but still not allowing myself to be beaten, I went to the army careers office which was next door to the RAF careers office. This time I passed. At last, the perseverance had finally paid off. It was 1980 and I was so excited that I'd managed to achieve something. I'd also learned an invaluable lesson, and that was to never give up! I was 17 years old, but inside I was still a child. Alcohol became a big part of army life and was the only thing that made me feel confident enough to socialise and join in with others. I was accepted into the RAOC (Royal Army Ordnance Corps) after passing a three day initial selection test held at Birmingham's Sutton Coldfield, where we were put through some basic fitness tests and a medical. I'd been well prepared for this as I was a keen runner and body builder, so I flew through the tests. We only had to do a few pull-ups, dips, sit-ups and a general fitness running test.

At the end of the selection weekend, we were asked to choose our preferred regiment. My choice was the Green Howards, but the recruitment officer persuaded me to join the RAOC. I wish that I'd stuck to my guns and insisted on the Green Howards as I needed the level of excitement and physical training the infantry offered. Before joining up, I was sent a travel warrant to start my training on 17 November 1980. I met a few of the lads at Camberley train station in Surrey to all got the bus into Deepcut where Blackdown Barracks was situated (now the infamous renamed Deepcut Barracks). This was where I was to spend the next three months, doing our basic training. As the bus approached, I could hear the sound of gun fire and loud voices shouting orders from the parade square. We spent our first day marching around the camp, trying to keep in step. Our first stop was the barber's where a really effeminate barber shaved the sides and back of our hair. Bearing in mind, this was the 1980s and a lot of the lads were into the fashion of the day, so they were devastated watching all their curls and locks fall to the ground. Most of the haircuts looked ridiculous after the barber had sheered us because some of the lads insisted on leaving as much hair on top as possible and just having it shaved around the edges. The army rules were that anything under your hat was yours, the rest was theirs. It was easier just to get the whole lot shaved off. In those days, having a shaved head meant you were either a skinhead, squaddie (soldier), or thug. We were then marched to the clothing store known as the Quartermasters. There we had to walk along the front of a long bench and have our new uniforms, kit and bedding items hurled at us until they were piled up so high that we couldn't see over the top.

Marching everywhere in ranks of three, dressed in all the fashions and bright colours of the 1980s, must have been a sight to see. One lad, called 'Punky', turned up wearing torn jeans with chains, safety pins and piercings through various body parts. We were expected to know our regimental numbers 'off by heart' by now, because we had been given a letter at the army careers office with them on when we'd sworn the oath.

I remember swearing my oath upstairs in the army careers office to a rather eccentric Major. He held a Bible in one hand, while reading out passages of the oath that I had to repeat back. During this very important part of enlisting, one of his lenses fell from his spectacles, landing on his desk. I burst out laughing and then struggled on, repeating the oath while desperately trying to stifle my giggling.

We were then taken to the Borneo platoon block where we were given our bed spaces. There were several other platoons situated in identical buildings nearby and we were always encouraged to compete against one another in competitions, sports and training.

Now it was over to the cookhouse, a huge, busy dining hall. It was a daunting sort of experience at first, with hundreds of people everywhere. The queues were enormous with lines of hungry men from various regiments and women from the Women's Royal Army Corps. One lone soldier in the dinner queue stood out from the crowd to me.

There was a trolley in the cookhouse where you scraped your plates and piled them up. Sometimes, if the staff were over busy, the pile got so high it would then come crashing to the floor. When it was me who put that final plate on top, causing it to topple, I used to get out fast so they wouldn't see who had sent them all smashing to the ground. There was always the sound of music coming from speakers situated around the cookhouse. I recall Neil Diamond's new release, *Love on the Rocks,* filling the air with such poignancy. Not long after breakfast, we'd be inspected outside the platoon block and then told to get changed into our PT kits for fitness training. Our kit consisted of long blue shorts, tee-shirts and black plimsolls if we were training in the gym.

If we were running, we wore khaki lightweight trousers, tee-shirts and boots. A few of us got stitches during the early morning runs, which wasn't surprising - seeing as we'd only eaten breakfast about an hour before. Missing breakfast is an offence in the army. If you collapse while on the parade square and it's discovered that you missed breakfast, you can be charged, although this is never done. It's one of those rules that remains in existence but isn't taken seriously.

Sometimes, we'd run in full combat gear which consisted of heavy camouflaged jackets and trousers, boots, ammunition pouches and carrying a 9lb self-loading rifle (SLR). I remember, during a run, one of the lads smashed head first into a lamppost when a young lady caught his eye from the roadside. We ran along the roads led by a physical training instructor (PTI). There'd be one at the front and one at the rear wearing an aluminous vests watching and directing traffic.

Some of our PTI's were a breed of their own. They were very over confident, full of themselves and very much full of their own importance. Years later, I met one of them again in Durham Prison.

The 12 weeks of basic training were great, I was always at the front of the ranks when we were out running and first at everything else too. Thanks to Dennis Shaw teaching me some self-defence techniques back home, I knew some Aikido moves too which we did as part of our 'battle' PT lessons. Later in life, I would gain a black belt in Aikido. One of our PTI's, Corporal Barley, who was from Wales, had a real evil streak. He and some of his sidekicks took us all for our swimming test at the Officer Training School at Sandhurst one Saturday morning. I was a non-swimmer, so I welcomed the lessons. To my horror though, we weren't there for a day out at the swimming baths. We were all lined up at the edge of the pool while one of the junior ranks, Lance Corporal Hawkings, demonstrated how easy it was to stay afloat by filling your lungs with air. Then Corporal Barley told all the non-swimmers to stand at the 12 foot end of the pool and then ordered us all to jump in and tread water for three minutes on his command. Totally petrified, we followed his orders and all jumped in. After all, we were starting to become brain washed by now, so we didn't question, we just did what we were ordered to do. As soon as we hit the water, we all started panicking as we fought to stay afloat, sinking and swallowing large gulps of water, frantically struggling not to drown. I could feel myself sinking lower and lower, desperately struggling to stay afloat. Then, myself and another lad, who was also panicking, decided to swim to the side of the pool, get out of the water and to hell with orders. One of the junior ranks, a Lance Corporal, who thought he was incredibly tough and God's gift, was screaming at us to jump back in. I ignored him, he was an idiot. Corporal Barley revealed to us later that in one of the last batches of recruits he took to the pool, one of the non-swimmers drowned "because he wouldn't stay still," he said. What a shame he hadn't disobeyed his orders like I had and got out of the pool.

We were barracked in (confined to camp) most nights, but I didn't drink then, so it didn't bother me. Then exactly three weeks into training, shocking news came over the radio announcing that John Lennon had been assassinated. One of my all-time favourite songs I was always playing at the time (*Just like*) *Starting Over,* was released only weeks before his death.

The Platoon Corporal in charge of us, Corporal Cooper, was a 'Jekyll and Hyde' character. He'd pay random visits to the block at all times of the night while worse for wear and get us to do change parades just for the hell of it. I know it was all part of the training, but he definitely had a screw loose.

Change parades would start with us all being ordered to stand outside our block in ranks of three. We would then be ordered to get changed into particular clothes and be back outside in the fastest time possible. The junior ranks would be pushing us down the stairs and screaming at us. Thinking of it now makes me giggle, but at the time I was scared stiff. I was more nervous than most others, who just took things in their stride.

One night we were told to get changed into full combats, helmets, wearing our respirators (gas masks) and be back downstairs as fast as possible carrying our mattresses on our shoulders. When we were all congregated back outside in the three ranks, we were taken for a run around the camp and across the parade square. What a sight we must have been. Without the corporal noticing, I unscrewed the canister from my respirator so I could take in large gulps of fresh air. Our respirators were used for Nuclear, Biological and Chemical (NBC) warfare training. This included entering a gas chamber where we were taken through a survival drill, consisting of several small tests. I'd been dreading what awaited us as we were taken across to the sinister looking brick building which had no windows - just a door.

We were all kitted out in our NBC suits (noddy suits) with our respirators in pouches. An NBC suit was a smock with hood and trousers which was worn over the uniform with the webbing on the outside and it was not the most comfortable thing to wear. There was a contraption in the centre of the chamber where a CS gas canister was ignited quickly filling the air with thick smoke. The drill required us to remove our respirators - just enough to eat a biscuit and drink some water - and replace them again. Unfortunately for me, when I replaced my respirator, the seal wasn't covering my face properly, so gas leaked though the sides choking me. At the end of the drill, we were all met at the door one at a time by Corporal Cooper where we had to remove our respirators completely and then answer a few questions such as number, rank and name. This was to get us used to the gas, the smell and the burning sensation of it.

By the time it was my turn to leave, my eyes were streaming and my face felt as though it was on fire, not to mention the uncontrollable coughing fit I had. One of the NCO's said, "Let him out, he's had enough". The next time I got a taste of CS gas like that was many years later, when I was sprayed by several police officers that I was wrestling with.

The dormitories housed 12 recruits and our daily routine began with roll call at 5.30am, where we would first of all make a bed pack which consisted of one blanket on top of a sheet, on top of a blanket, with a blanket wrapped around them and our pillows placed on top. We left one sheet on the bed with the top cover folded half way down.

Our metal mess tins, from which we ate our food when we were out in the field on exercise, had to be immaculate. Boots had to be 'bulled' (spit and polished with a rag) with layers and layers of polish, soaked overnight, and then buffed the next day.

One of our daily routines was to take turns buffing the floor. The buffer was a heavy metal attachment on the end of a solid wooden broom handle. We all learned how to iron too which we did each night to be ready for the next morning as well as polishing the bathroom basins, baths and taps.

One of the main tasks at the very start of our training was to burn our boots. In those days, we were issued with two pairs. Both had pimples down and around the sides. One pair was used for everyday use so we only had to 'bull' the toe cap. The other pair were our 'best boots' which had to have an overall shine. To get this shine, we had to spend one night with lit candles and spoons. You heated the back of the spoon then pushed it across the boot melting all the pimples until your boots were entirely smooth. It was a lengthy and boring process, but we all sat around having a good 'crack' while doing it. I flew through basic training with flying colours achieving the highest fitness assessment score of 178 which was calculated from how many push-ups we could do, how many sit-ups we could do and so on. I remember doing almost one hundred inclined sit ups on a wooden bench which were counted out by one of my mates. At some point, Corporal Barley intervened and told me to stop and to stand to attention. He said, "Well done, Honeywell". That was one of the biggest boosts I had ever had, but not as much as when he later announced all the individual scores in the changing room. Deliberately missing my name out, he shouted, "Has anyone's name not been read out?" I raised my arm.

"Stand up, Honeywell!" he said. He read out my score of 178 as being the highest ever achieved in the platoon for which I received a rapturous applause and the bumps.

It was so strange how far I had come along in my physical fitness since school. Only two years earlier, I was so terrified of taking part in any kind of sports or PT activities at school that I would deliberately leave my gym kit at home - even accepting that I would be slippered for it. All that changed after the same teacher who used to slipper me, one day praised me instead. I now wonder whether my school years would have been different had I been praised more often. A confident team player? Runner? Confident boy? Quite possibly.

The Navy, Army and Air Force Institutes (NAAFI), was the local shop and bar on the camp. Some weekends, other regiments would visit and whenever the Parachute Regiment turned up, there was always trouble. We had plastic beer glasses; the sort of thing which we tend to associate with today's culture, yet this was 1981. When we were given guard duty, we would wear our combats and sleep over in the guardroom through the night, taking turns with our 'stag' duty. I hated being woken up every four hours to go and patrol the camp carrying pick-axe handles. Some drunk would always try and test you on their way back from the pub. Once Borneo platoon reached the end of the twelve weeks basic training, it was celebrated with a passing out parade. Families and friends were invited to watch us all proudly marching in our number two's (best uniforms). It was a proud, emotional day. My mother came with friends, and Dennis and Janet Shaw came along with their kids.

We all received weekend leave passes, after which we returned to take up our trade training as supply specialists (store men/women). The Sergeant running the course referred to himself as God. I took an instant dislike to him. There was another Sergeant who was assisting him who came from Middlesbrough. He was nice man, but showed me up one day by pointing out something I got wrong to the whole class which brought back bad school memories. The truth is, I hated all the classroom work and being cooped up inside doing a job civilians do. When I was running around during basic training, I loved every minute of it - even if I was scared at times of some of the Military Training Instructors, (MTI's) but it suited me.

One weekend, I went on a little jaunt to London, where I soaked up the delights of Soho amongst the seedy strip clubs and extortionate bars. I was late getting back that Monday morning after sleeping rough at a train station in London.

This was a period of my life when my attitudes started to change towards authority figures who thought they were God! The Sergeant who thought he was God disliked me almost as much as I disliked him and I didn't try to hide it. At end of the three week trade training, when he announced we'd all passed our exams, when he deliberately pointed out to the whole class that I had only got through by the 'skin of my teeth'. Some were emotional and hugging one another after passing. I looked on, detached from the rest of them and completely unconcerned about any of it. I was relieved it had ended, but I had no emotion whatsoever, except a sudden realisation that I was in the wrong regiment.

The past weeks of trade training under an egotistical Sergeant and his sidekick increased my hatred for classrooms and exams even more. Being a Supply Specialist wasn't the most exciting job, so I spent several months trying to transfer to the Infantry. I wasn't supported at all with my application but instead just met with sniggers and petty comments by bigoted admin workers. They eventually refused to take my application any further forward. It was at that point, I lost all interest in the RAOC, the army and any desire to conform.

Soon after completing the first part of our trade training, we were then sent to RAF Leconfield near Beverley which is about ten miles from Hull. Here, we were to do the second part of our trade training which was to gain our Heavy Goods Vehicle (HGV) licence. This was an expected part of our Supply Specialist role. It was an excellent opportunity. The training took us through learning to drive a car if we couldn't already drive, to driving a *Land Rover,* then to HGV level when you could drive large *Bedford* army trucks. I was still teetotal so I felt like an outcast to a point but this had been a real bonus during basic training because I had the upper hand in always being fitter than the rest. I was now part of a different culture - a drinking culture.

Each morning, we all had to congregate for roll call inside an aircraft hangar before heading off for our driving lessons. I'd been in many of these places as a child. We were all designated a driving instructor. Mine was a rather tough looking Sergeant who was towards the latter end of his army service. With our instructors, we then went through a daily drill of checking tyre pressures, checking the engine and so on. All this is beyond me now. I wouldn't have a clue. For some reason, I just couldn't see it through. I didn't like my instructor's manner either. He was gruff and arrogant, but he wasn't the worst I'd met. I was so nervous driving, I stalled the car at a major roundabout in Doncaster one day. It was so busy it freaked me out.

A few days later, after roll call, I went into the office and confessed that I should be wearing glasses but didn't have any. This was my way of getting out of it. I was then Returned To Unit (RTU'd), but it was what I had wanted. It would also be yet another lifelong regret. Being a non-driver has caused me so many difficulties over the years.

Not long after, we were given our postings. That was when things went rapidly downhill for me. I was posted to 10 Ordnance Support Battalion just outside a small town in Wiltshire called Devizes. Nowadays, I'd be fascinated by this village as it's purported to be one of the most haunted towns in the UK, but when I was 18, I was bored senseless with the place. I didn't like the daily '9-5' work routine in the stores, or where I was posted, nor did I like the regiment.

Once I had transferred to Devizes, I soon started drinking and smoking heavily; it was such a tedious place, where drinking was the order of the day. We had money, local girls on tap, and we made the most of it. This would be the downfall of my army career and the start of my reckless lifestyle for many years to come. Alcohol got the better of me, so much so, that I got to the stage of missing the morning roll call and getting someone else to answer to my name. I had gone from being a teetotal, non-smoking super fit soldier, with a promising army career ahead of me during basic training, to a drunken, chain smoking individual without a care in the world for anyone and rebellious against authority.

All my wages went on beer and fags. These were things I'd never done before, but I wanted to fit in and felt as though drinking would help me become 'one of the lads'. It was my alcohol consumption that would become my nemesis. Before joining the army, I was teetotal and for someone who is prone to depression, consuming alcohol was the worst thing I could do. It led to me going AWOL Absent Without Leave (AWOL), which I always did while under the influence of alcohol. One night I took a taxi all the way from Devizes to my home in Eston. As the months passed, I became increasingly home sick and bored to death. I started going AWOL on a regular basis, where I would go back home to Middlesbrough, then two or three days later, return to the barracks thinking that I could carry on where I'd left off. Each time, I would be hauled in front of the Commanding Officer (C.O.)to be given my punishment. During the days leading up to this I would be placed under 'close arrest' which basically meant I was confined to the barracks. When my time came to be dealt with, I'd be anxiously waiting outside the C.O.s office standing in the middle of two escorts. The door would burst open and a warrant officer would shout, "Quick march!" I was marched in at a faster than normal pace into the office, around the front of the desk where the C.O. was sitting to our left, and came to attention. Then I would wait for the order – "Left turn!" so that I was facing the C.O. One day I turned right by mistake so my back was facing the C.O. He then had to shout "Left turn!" twice until I was facing him. I could see out the corner of my eye the Lance Corporal to my right desperately trying to stop laughing. I could see his shoulders going up and down and could hear him trying to control his giggling. I was given a fine and told to carry on with my duties. It seemed like a long time in that office, but we had a good laugh about it afterwards. This didn't stop me going AWOL though and after going absent again, I was given my first ever taste of prison in the army glasshouse (detention) which was a short sharp shock that would shock me to the core. The glasshouse is no picnic. The difference between a military prison and a civilian prison is that you can be locked up in a military prison for offences that breach military rules, but are not necessarily criminal offences.

Offences in the army can include going AWOL, being drunk and disorderly, and anything that they think warrants a stint in jail. I once saw a recruit being swiftly marched to the guardroom carrying a mattress on his shoulder; he had been arrested because he had love bites all over his neck. At least if I'd been arrested for this, I would have felt it had been worth it. The difference is of course, once you've done your sentence, you can return to normal duties and 'soldier on' as they say, whereas in 'civvy' street, you will struggle to live a normal life after being convicted.

A term in the glasshouse, was always said to make you a better soldier because of the brutal regime. Although Colchester is the main glasshouse in the military, each camp has their own guardroom with cells and some are run like Colchester. Military prison is nicknamed the glasshouse because everything inside is polished and buffed like glass until you can see your face in it.

The first experience of seeing inside a military prison cell was when I was ten and we were living at RAF Leeming. My father took me to the guardroom one day where he showed me a small, bare, cold room which had a solid wooden bench for a bed and at the head of the bench was one folded grey blanket. The barred window was so high up that anyone who had to spend time in there would never be able to reach to see out. It served no purpose other than to allow a glimmer of light through. The floor was like glass, gleaming from the reflection of the light coming through the bars. There was a hatch on the door which was used to pass food to prisoners. I remember feeling shocked at how severe it all looked and was trying to imagine how terrible it must be for anyone to have to spend a night in this grim place. Little did I know, that eight years later, I would be locked inside one myself. My second experience as an observer was when I was stationed at Blackdown Barracks. I kept seeing a young soldier being marched around everywhere at a mad pace while being screamed at by the Provost Sergeant following behind him. The soldier had his hair shaved and was stripped of all identity; he wasn't wearing his beret or any jacket; he just had his khaki shirt, lightweights and boots without laces. What had really caught my eye though, was the empty coffin leaning against the guardroom wall outside. When I asked about it, I was told it was because the prisoner had attempted suicide. He was being 'beasted' around like an animal because he was depressed enough to make an attempt on his own life; the coffin was to make him think twice about doing it again. Provost staff (regimental police) were a joke really; they took themselves far too seriously and always dressed to impress. Their hat peaks and boots shone like glass. If the peaks of their hats weren't slashed, they did it themselves to make themselves look meaner. A slashed peak is where the lining of the hat is cut and the peak is pushed further in so it fits low over the bridge of the nose. If anyone else did this, they were charged for damaging military property.

It was now my turn to be 'beasted' and I was soon to get the shock of my life.

6. The 'Glasshouse'

The thing that landed me in the glasshouse first time around was after I deserted while away on exercise in Denmark. I was later told that if you do a 'runner' from camp, it's AWOL, but if you're away on exercise it's classed as desertion. Apparently, you can still be shot for it, but I knew that wasn't going to happen. En route to Denmark, we all stayed over at *Brize-Norton*, ready to fly out the next morning. We all boarded the *Hercules* aeroplane. I took a supply of beer for the journey by filling my ammunition pouches with cans of lager. I noticed there were some sick bags for anyone who felt the need to vomit but I wasn't going to drink on the plane so I wouldn't need one. They were exactly like the ones my father used to bring home for my travel sickness when I was a kid. I was excited to be going abroad for the first time, we had all been given our wages in Danish Krone and I intended to make the most of it.

Once we arrived, the thing that struck me most was how clean all the roads and streets were everywhere. At the barracks where we were to stay for the next six weeks, I noticed that the Danish soldiers were a not as formal as we were. They all had shoulder length hair and walked around playing with yo-yo's. We were barracked-in most nights and worked most of the day, we spent what was left of our evenings watching television and generally being even more bored to tears than back at our base in England. We did get some time away though; on our first night in Denmark, we all headed to Copenhagen for drinks and a traditional visit to the red-light district. I lost my virginity that night which cost me 200 Krone for half an hour. I was ushered into this chic looking boudoir by a stunning blonde Danish lady. After that night, we were all barracked in night after night, until I'd had enough. One day, I told the Corporal in charge that I had to go to the bank to draw some cash out; I was, in fact heading for the train station and then for Copenhagen, where I went on the run for a week. I spent my days drinking in bars and my nights, sleeping rough. Looking back, I have no idea why I wanted to put myself through that kind of ordeal. I even got a job for a time working as a dish washer at the Capital's Train Station restaurant. I dropped myself in it though when I told one of the waitresses that I was a deserter, who then told the manager, who of course fired me. I don't know why I told her I was a deserter. I suppose I thought it would impress her. After a week, the money ran out and I was exhausted, hungry and missing life's little luxuries, so I turned myself in to the Danish police who escorted me to the British Embassy. At the Embassy, I was met by a real English gentleman, who was obviously in charge and, I think, was either an army officer or he had been one. He ushered me into a huge luxurious office which had leather chairs and polished tables. We talked for a while when he suddenly asked, "Have you got any cigarettes?" He handed me a packet of about six *John Players* cigarettes he had taken from his pocket. I thought it was a nice gesture. He probably realised that I had been living like a tramp during my stint on the run and took pity on me. I also noticed, on the table in front of me, a tall plastic container full of complimentary cigarettes for visitors. When he left the office to ring the army Provost crew to come and collect me, I helped myself to a handful, stuffing them in my jacket pocket. When the Provost crew turned up, they all strutted in led by the ever arrogant, Sergeant Major Malone. He was an imposing presence who liked to try and intimidate people with his large physique and even larger mouth.

I was quite embarrassed though, because when the 'motley crew' ordered me to turn out my pockets, there I was, taking out a handful of the cigarettes I'd just helped myself to while the Embassy gentleman was out of the room. I looked over to him but he didn't even 'bat an eyelid'. *He's a true gentleman*, I thought - unlike the rabble that I had to travel back to camp with. I may have been a law breaker and a nuisance over the years, but I have always been as polite and courteous as I can. I've never acted like a Neanderthal, unlike many that I have had the misfortune to spend time with. The 'motley crew' took me back to camp where I was met with hostility and contempt from others who didn't know me and weren't even in the same regiment. It's always easy to target a vulnerable person when you're amongst a group of other likeminded people, but they fail to understand that anyone can one day find themselves on the wrong side of the law.

I hadn't broken the law, however, I had broken army rules. There is a massive difference because when you're under arrest in the army, just like the soldier I saw at Blackdown Barracks, you're marched everywhere at a ridiculously fast pace and stripped of all identity. You're not allowed to wear your hat or have laces in your boots; you're not allowed to associate with or speak to your comrades, because you've 'supposedly' 'disgraced the regiment'. I remember standing outside the C.O.s office awaiting to hear my fate for the rest the Denmark exercise, when I heard the song, *One Day In Your Life* by Michael Jackson playing on someone's radio and thinking how much I liked the dulcet sound of this ballad.

An officer escorted me to what was to be my place of work for the next few days. It was a large field where they had been serving meals to the troops. There were hundreds of large dirty pots, pans and kitchen utensils scattered around, cigarette butts everywhere and a general mess. It is ironic that this would later become my type of employment in civilian life when I was released from prison in 1985.

Nearby, there were dormitories where I could see other squaddies milling around inside and suffering from the boredom that had driven me to desert in the first place. I had been given Restriction Of Privileges, (ROP's) and put to work as a general 'dogs body' which consisted of washing, sweeping and running errands. This sort of punishment used to be called jankers or fatigues. Whenever they got the opportunity, the other squaddies would try to humiliate me by throwing their fag butts on the floor outside their windows for me to sweep up, or by directing childish and pathetic remarks at me.

A few days later I was flown back to Gatwick airport in a *Hercules*. Apart from the pilot, there was only myself and a young lady from the Women's Royal Army Corps (WRAC) on the plane. Before boarding the plane, Malone passed my files to her asking if she would look after them during the flight until we arrived at Gatwick where I was to be met by the regiment's police. She looked petrified. Once I was back on UK soil, I was arrested and taken back to Devizes camp and straight to the guardroom where I was immediately locked up in what was just a small wooden hut. I lay awake most of the night planning my escape which would have been quite easy. I was allowed to come and go to the toilet. The windows had no bars on them so I could have easily climbed through and slid down the side of the wall. I could have then crawled underneath the guardroom (which was raised on stilts) and then made my escape. In the end, I decided to just accept my fate instead - as I always had - whenever I was in trouble with the law. I would always accept my punishment. Never did I have a problem with the police, lawyers or prison officers.

Back at camp the next morning, I was quickly marched in front of the commanding officer, flanked by two Lance Corporals at either side of me. We stood to attention until instructed to stand at ease. Lieutenant Colonel Champion read out my name and number, "24598031: Private Honeywell?", "Yes Sir!" I replied. He added, "You have been charged with going absent without leave."

Once all the formalities were over and done with, he gave me 27 days detention and ordered me to 'soldier on' once I was released. To 'soldier on' meant that once you had paid your dues, you could return to normal duties. It is a shame that the civilian criminal justice system and society doesn't work in the same way.

I was taken by *Land Rover* on what seemed like an eternity, to Warminster, escorted by Sergeant Mac, an ex-paratrooper, whom I had befriended and had always admired. We used to go running together every day, but now he was escorting me to jail. I knew he didn't like doing it. He was real old school, with a huge handlebar moustache. He had great spirit and toughness. Entering the gates of the Warminster School of Infantry Camp was quite daunting. Sergeant Mac turned to me and said, "Just get your head down and take your punishment, Honeywell, then come out and start again." I could feel the anxiety inside me increasing as the *Land Rover* neared the guardroom, where a Scots Guard Sergeant stood waiting by the entrance, clutching a pace stick. I was escorted through to the guardroom which had a desk to the left where one of the jailers was sitting.

The place reeked of polish and fear. On the other side of the room was a large window and through it, I could see a large room with three beds in a row. The floor was immaculately polished and gleamed from the reflection of the sun that squeezed through a skylight.

I was told to stand to attention at one the end of the desk while all the formalities were discussed with Sergeant Mac. I really had no idea what awaited me. The guards who we had to refer to as 'staff' were garrison police - a feared arm of the military with a reputation for brutality. There was a Scottish Sergeant who met us at the entrance, who happened to be a real gentleman, actually. There was a Brummy Lance Corporal from the Irish Guards who was a decent enough bloke and hadn't time for all the 'army bullshit'. There was also a Liverpudlian Corporal who I liked most of all because he didn't throw his weight around. He was so laid back that he seemed more like one of us. Then there was a psychotic Black Watch Corporal called Smudge Smith, who I despised. He had a real Machiavellian streak and personal issues that he would take out on us. Then, there was a short Corporal with a real case of 'Napoleon syndrome' who tried to use his loud voice to scare people because he had no physical presence at all.

While I was standing to attention waiting to be processed, just for a split second, he caught me glancing over towards his direction, at which point he ran over to me and screamed, "Are you looking at me!!!?" We were almost nose to nose - at least we would have been, had he been tall enough. "You listen to me! when I say go! you left turn!, run through the back!, get in your cell! and slam the door shut! Do you understand!!!?"

I nodded. I knew from that moment that it was going to be hell, and that it was going to be a very long 27 days. I was dreading what lay ahead. …"Go!" the Corporal screamed, making me jump out of my skin. I pivoted to the left, slamming my right heel into the ground bringing myself to attention. As fast as I could, I ran through the corridor behind me to a cell situated at the far right and slammed the door behind me. This would be a sound that I would become accustomed to over the years. My cell, which was situated in a corner at the rear of the building, was near some showers it looked just like the cell my father once shown me when I was ten. It had the same heavy metal door with a hatch to pass food through, but we ate our meals at the cookhouse, so it was never used for this purpose. The walls and door were painted bright red, which I'm sure had been deliberately painted that colour to make us go insane. However, we didn't spend that much time in our cells because we were always running, marching or cleaning the guardroom. Each morning we were up at 5.00am, ready to start the day with an early morning run through the nearby woods, carrying a huge, heavy log on our shoulders, followed by a cold shower. As we ran, the log was bouncing on my bony shoulder, causing immense pain. The rest of the day was spent polishing and cleaning the guardroom and getting our kit ready for the next morning's inspection. The guards would sometimes get us to do random things, such as marching us up and down and around the camp. The only laugh we ever got, which only lasted for a short while, was with a large built Corporal from the Coldstream Guards who was temporarily brought in. He used to make us burst out laughing when he shouted orders at us. It gave us some sort of relief and helped us get through because he too, saw the funny side.

Every morning, the duty officer for the day would strut in to inspect us, our beds, and kit, which was all neatly laid out on top of our beds. Each night, we had to polish the peak of our hat which sat on top of our bed blocks just like we had made in basic training, except in here, they had to measure exactly nine inches by nine inches and if it was slightly askew, it would be hurled to the floor.

Our best boots and shoes, which we spent hours polishing until they were gleaming, were carefully laid out along the side of the bed. Down the centre of the bed, our shirts and trousers were also folded and pressed to exact measurements. Then, at the bottom, was our toothpaste, soap, and cutlery positioned in a uniformed manner. We scrubbed the paint off our toothpaste tubes and shoe polish tins until they were silver. If the duty officer was one of those who had a point to prove, he would bring a ruler to measure our folded up shirts and blankets. It was pathetic. On my second day there, I was marched to the medical office. I automatically sat with the other patients. The short red faced guard came across to me teeth clenched: "Get up!", he growled. Once I had been medically examined and told that I was fit for detention, I was back outside being screamed at, "Quick march! About turn! Left turn! Right turn! About turn!"

I noticed two women walk past us with pushchairs, shaking their heads and frowning at the guard. I suddenly stopped and said: "Fuck it!" The shouting and screaming continued and had eventually got to me. I don't mind admitting this but I started to cry. However, I had started to accept that breaking rules came at a price and taking punishment was all part and parcel of it. We were allowed two cigarettes a day, which we had to smoke while standing to attention. Each day was spent being humiliated in one way or another which exceeded punishment. Smudge Smith grabbed me by the throat one morning, pushed me against the cell wall and squeezed my windpipe because I had got up too early. I had already got up, made my bed block and had my kit all laid out earlier than usual and he didn't approve. He would often turn nasty, then shortly afterwards, call me through to the office and offer me one of his own cigarettes.

I always wished that I had met some of the guards after my release. They always seemed to forget that time stands still for no man and one day, most prisoners do get released. Some of the guards were scum of the earth and not interested in doing a good job. They were just there to vent their pathetic personal issues on vulnerable prisoners. I was supposed to be the one who had disgraced the army, but at least I had never been a bully or preyed on the weak. One of them explained to me that prisoners who they knew had come from broken homes, were easier to crack. When my sentence finally ended, I was collected by one of the drivers and taken back to Devizes. It wasn't long before I got into debt and was borrowing money from everyone. Every penny I earned went on beer and fags, so I borrowed more and more to feed my new addictions. Every night, I went out on the town, around the local pubs, drinking myself into a stupor because there was just nothing else to do on camp. The boredom was too much, so I just drank myself into oblivion every night.

Because of my recent experiences in the glasshouse, they decided to put my newly acquired talents to good use, and offered me a job working as a regimental policeman. This was an easy number and it was something that suited me. I had always wanted to be a policeman when I was a young boy and throughout my teens too. The only thing that prevented me from joining the police was that I had no qualifications at the time. If I had, I most certainly would have joined the police force. This seems so bizarre to me now, knowing all that's happened since, and probably quite alarming to most people who know me too. I remember, having an interview with an Inspector at York Police Station in 1983, when I was told that I needed five O-levels, but I felt that getting those was beyond my capabilities.

That year, I ended up on the opposite side of the law and back at York Police Station on criminal charges, at the beginning of a journey that would leave me with massive regrets to this day. Being a regimental policeman, I had to do a stint guarding the gate, which meant stopping cars and doing random checks on vehicles as they entered the camp. Some wouldn't stop so I made a note of the registration number and reported them. Jim was a former police officer, a fearless man of large stature who was in charge of me - I really enjoyed working with him. He showed me how to direct traffic one day, when the army held a gala day. Jim wasn't liked by many others though, because he rubbed people up the wrong way. This was a period where I seemed to be settling down, but then the debt started getting worse and my behaviour was becoming more and more erratic.

The next time I went AWOL, was the last time. It was only a few weeks since my last detention and before my feet even touched the ground, I was back in the glasshouse for another 14 days, going through all the same routine as before. My second stint in the glasshouse wasn't as bad as the first time; it was as though they had realised that I was just a lost cause, and that no matter how much they bawled and shouted at me, I was going home anyway. One day, while I was polishing the floor, the door burst open and in marched Jim, followed by Sergeant Mac, barking, "Left, right, left right left right!"

I couldn't believe my eyes, seeing Jim carrying a suitcase, his single Lance Corporal stripe hung from his sweater where it had been ripped off. I can't recall what had led to this, but I do remember that he never succumbed to the guards' bully tactics; the Black Watch guard, Smudger, asked me to 'have a word' with him to try and get him to 'toe the line'. They had done this with a prisoner I'd spent my time with during my 27 days, who threatened to kick my head in if I didn't 'screw the bob'. *If only I'd had Jim's strength of character*, I thought.

Years later, while I was in prison doing my five year stretch, I saw Jim on *Countdown,* the television quiz programme and I later heard that he had died.

By now, the army had had enough of me messing about, so they 'drummed' me out after just one year and 17 days. It would become one of the biggest regrets of my life, but it didn't stop me doing foolish things throughout my life. I still believe, that had the RAOC allowed me to transfer to an infantry regiment when I asked them, I would have stayed in the army. The RAOC hated me but I hated them even more.

7. First Offence

After I left the army, I felt that society owed me and it was all society's fault that I was failing in everything I did. I had a huge chip on my shoulder and every intention of wreaking havoc. I was 19 and had just started carrying knives. Although I have pinpointed when my behaviour began to change; the reason I transformed from being a timid, quiet, shy - although disturbed boy, into a persistently violent, knife carrying offender, is more complex.

I may have stolen, and been fired from my job for it, and I know I'd screwed up my army career, but I wasn't a violent thug. So where did that come from? Sometimes I still struggle to answer this myself, but I can clearly see that there were worrying behavioural changes during my early teens. However, it was after I became a heavy drinker that I started committing serious, violent offences fuelled with 'Dutch courage'. This happened almost straight after being kicked out of the army.

Until then, the only bad thing I had done under the influence of alcohol was going AWOL. I left the army much tougher and more confident, and because I had done some time in a military prison, I thought I was a bit of a 'tough guy'. Part of the reason I was a knife carrier, was the same reason why today's youths carry knives; because a big part of me felt that I needed to be in control and gain respect through instilling fear. I felt the need to protect myself from being attacked by gangs. Some young men feel that carrying a weapon makes them a man; powerful and in control, as I did. For most of my young life, I carried weapons, usually knives, and sometimes more than one, they made me feel that I was in charge, and in control over other aspects of my life, that I had no control over. When young men carry weapons, they can emulate their gangster role models, like Ronnie Kray or Al Capone. This was a huge part of my transition from being just a bad boy. This developed when I began reading books about famous criminals and The Mafia. I was first inspired by a book I had read about the Kray twins, called *Profession of violence: The rise and fall of the Kray Twins*. I saw them as the 'Robin Hood's' of their day; I saw them as people who were well respected, and should be aspired to. I connected immediately, with their rebellion against the army and their stint in the glasshouse. I related to the fact that they saw the Provost staff as a total joke as I had, but respected war heroes and gentlemen officers.

I started writing to them and received a reply shortly after my first letter from both Reg and Ron. This was exciting, I got a real buzz from it. I used to watch gangster films and documentaries all the time, I remember being glued to the television watching a series called *Gangster Chronicles*, which was a history of 'organised crime' in 1920's and 30's America. It was their style, fearsome reputations, and their defiance towards authority that inspired me. I decided that I was going to teach people a lesson in respect if anyone tried to belittle me and this first surfaced when I committed my first offence. It is of no surprise to me now, that I went off the rails.

After being kicked out of the army in 1981, I had returned to Teesside, where nothing had changed. There were still high unemployment figures, and a lot of men were out of work, men who had always thought that they had jobs for life. The sight of men covered in black dirt walking through the streets after a hard shift at work was becoming a less familiar sight. I had now blown my army career and was back in Middlesbrough, my tail between my legs and a less than favourable reference, hardly worth the paper it was written on. I had screwed up big time and paved the way for a long and arduous journey throughout life where I would end up working in dead end jobs and, going nowhere.

Oh, how bad choices we make in the early part of our lives can so easily map out our destinies. If only we had the foresight to see the consequences of our actions, feel the pain we will one day cause ourselves and inflict on others. I would have given anything to be able to live a life with a clean slate, to be able to choose a job I wanted, and to be able to work towards a career without the worry of my past spoiling it, but what is done is done. The oppressive atmosphere in Teesside, created by high unemployment, was increasing. On top of this, recent years had affected my mother and I badly, so we decided to leave the area. In 1983, we moved to her hometown of York. We managed to get a house exchange through what was then, Langbaurgh Borough Council.

Another family had wanted to move to Grangetown from York, so it was a straight swap. We moved to Harrington Avenue in Tang Hall, to start a new life - or so we thought. There were so many repairs that needed doing to our new, shabby council house and after some persuasion, we managed to get York Council to do something about it. It was evident that York Council was a different kettle of fish to the council in Teesside. Before, when it had come to asking for basic repairs to be done, we had never had this sort of resistance from the council. Eventually, they did the job that they were supposed to do, but it was clear to both my mother and myself, that it had been a mistake moving to York. The house was pre-war and had a beck just outside the back garden, which used to rise up in the winter, bringing rats and mice into the garden. We were always having to get rid of spiders and other creepy crawlies around the house too, which started to get us down. It was a typical example of us thinking that 'the grass would be greener' on the other side - only for it to turn out to be not greener, but a nightmare instead.

As the days and weeks passed, we both became more unhappy. I started going out and drinking a lot, but I enjoyed the night life. Despite feeling low, I tried to lead a normal life and managed to find a job at Russell's Restaurant, as a cleaner. I was always restless and hyper though, I always looked for excitement and was never satisfied with having a normal, daily routine. My drinking was causing me to get deeper, and deeper into depression.

North Easterners, were treated with suspicion by a lot of York residents, and understandably so; there had been a lot of trouble during race meetings and at weekends when gangs came through to get wasted on booze. One day, a huge fight broke out between rival gangs in Bootham, in the middle of the street, a bicycle was hurled through a shop window and passers-by were left terrified.

When I tell these stories to people, they are shocked to hear that such mindless violence could ever occur in such a beautiful city. It is outsiders that cause it and York has had its fair share of trouble as a result of gangs, hell bent on wreaking havoc, from other parts of the country. It was a minority, as always, who did this and then left a trail of destruction behind them when they returned home. There was a nightclub called The *Old World* in the early 80's where on entry, you were asked where you were from. If you had a North East accent, you were refused entry. However, if you could prove that you lived and worked in York, you were allowed in. I used take my pay slips everywhere with me as most pubs and clubs also had this same rule. One day, my mother and I walked into a local shop where she asked the owner a simple question, he, in return gave her a snotty reply. This experience, amongst other things, had started to build up inside me now. We had been messed about by the council, certain individuals from the so called 'upper echelons' of society who seemed to have taken over York, spoke to us as though we were beneath them and I'd had enough.

Now, with a huge chip on my shoulder, I spent part of the night drinking in the *Spotted Cow* in Walmgate, ruminating over everything that had happened since we had moved to York, and how everything had gone wrong in our lives. I decided to take revenge on the shop keeper who had been rude to my mother. I went back to that shop to rob it. Wearing a black balaclava and clutching a large knife I'd bought in Middlesbrough, I threatened the shopkeeper with the knife and tried to make him hand over money from the till. He panicked and I left the shop without any money. I had done what I had wanted to do; that was enough for me.

The next day, it was all over the *York Press,* which is ironic now; since then, I have written for the newspaper many times. Several days later, while visiting friends in Middlesbrough, I confessed to them. They persuaded me to hand myself in to the police. The police later told me, that I'd never have been caught had I not confessed, but this didn't bother me. I knew that what I'd done was wrong and I was prepared to take my punishment. I waited at my friend's house that night for detectives to arrive, they seemed to take forever.

Eventually, two officers turned up, arrested me and took me back to South Bank Police Station. I was led to the reception area, told to stand at the front desk and give my name and details to the desk Sergeant. I was searched and asked to empty my pockets where all my belongings such as my wallet, money, and comb were all placed on the desk, and then listed, I signed for them, so that I could collect them later.

My belt was removed and I was taken into another room where my fingerprints were taken. An officer held of one of my forefingers then pressed and rolled it across a black ink pad. Then, while still holding on, rolled it on to a sheet of white paper which illustrated which fingerprint goes where. Then he pressed both thumbs into the ink and then on to the paper. I always tensed my fingers, but they are supposed to be relaxed to take prints, it used to take several attempts to get it right, the police must have thought that I was doing it on purpose. Once I'd been finger printed, I was taken along a smelly, dingy corridor which housed several cells. Someone was hammering on his cell door shouting, "'Boss, Boss! Can I make a phone call!?"

I was told to take off my shoes which, were then left outside the cell door. Police custody is one of the worst stages of the arrest process because it's like being in solitary confinement – something that I would one day become acquainted with. I was locked in a smelly old cell which had a lingering stench of sweat, food, and decay. The walls and doors were daubed with years of graffiti, the bed was a solid wooden bench with two carefully folded grey woollen blankets sat on top of it. I used one of the blankets as a pillow as there wasn't a proper one. The cell windows were made of thick, frosted glass that offered no view of anything outside my four walls, and because it was permanently dark inside, there was no way of knowing what time of the day it was. Every half hour or so, I would hear the spy hole cover being moved as they kept checking on me. All there was to do all day was sleep, which was only interrupted when my solicitor turned up to go through my statement with me. Whatever time of day you were arrested, even if it was in the early hours of the morning, a duty solicitor would be called out to see you if you requested one. After going through my statement, my solicitor tried to get me bail, which was at the discretion of the duty police sergeant. Their decisions were based on the likelihood that you would do a runner, or if emotions in the community were running so high that you should be kept in for your own safety. I was kept in, as I was being transferred to York the next day.

When you're waiting to be transferred somewhere, it's a long and mind numbing wait, but once you're on the move and sat in that vehicle, a huge relief comes over you because you're out of those dreadful cells, even if you are handcuffed throughout the entire journey. I was collected by two police officers from York the next day. I don't remember what time of day it was when they arrived, but it seemed like an eternity to wait for them. One of them was from Teesside, so he'd taken the opportunity to visit his hometown. On the long journey back to York, I was handcuffed to him in the back of an unmarked police car and we had a bit of banter on the way. I was surprised that they were so easy going, and I remember thinking that they were actually okay.

As we travelled along Normanby Trunk Road, we were pulled over by the police. It was comical; they were accusing the officers I was with of running a red light, and clearly trying it on. The copper that I was cuffed to raised our hands, showing him the handcuffs. "We're escorting a prisoner," he said.

The red faced young copper apologised and sheepishly walked back to his car, his tail between his legs. I creased up laughing when the copper handcuffed to me muttered an insult at the young copper, which I cannot repeat.

Back at York Police Station, I was questioned by detectives then the next day, taken back to our house in Tang Hall. I was handcuffed to one of them while he, and one of his colleagues searched my bedroom to recover the weapon and balaclava. They confiscated those, and an SLR army issue rifle magazine, which I had held on to as a souvenir from my army days. This was classed as a weapon, and added to my record. I was just relieved that my mother was out that day, it would have upset her seeing me handcuffed to a huge copper.

My mother couldn't understand why I had gone from being such a quiet, stable, nice lad, to a criminal overnight. She also took offence at the detective telling her one day, that I was evil. He had based his opinion on the two days he'd known me.

The next day, I appeared before York Magistrate's Court, where my solicitor was certain that I would get bail this time, as it was my first offence. A group of us were appearing in court that day, so we were all handcuffed to one another and then taken to a white minibus where we sat at the back in two rows. When we were handcuffed to one other, the person to the right would have his right arm cuffed to the other person's right arm so his right arm was pulled across his body. The idea of this, was to make it difficult for us to make a run for it. As we drove through the streets of York, a real old school bobby, and one of our escorts, suddenly said to me, "Were you in the army then, Honeywell?"

"Yes"

"What regiment were you in?" he asked.

"RAOC," I answered.

"Oh, so you weren't in the army then!" he quipped.

The others gave a snigger as though they could have had even the slightest inclination what we were talking about. I just laughed. I didn't take offence at the old bobby's joke, I knew he was trying to keep everyone's spirits lifted. I guessed he would have had some stories to tell if he'd had half the chance!

One of the things that did stood out to me was how the officers and prisoners, bantered with one another. The police had obviously dealt with these individuals regularly and both parties had struck up this bizarre familiarity. The others thought it highly amusing that I had handed myself in to the police. They were even more entertained when one of the others asked the old school bobby, "Would he have been caught if he hadn't handed himself in?", to which the answer was, no. They all sniggered like school children. I was in the presence of what I considered, real morons, as the very thought of possessing any conscience was beyond them. I was sat next to an Asian police officer, which was a rare sight in those days and not so common these days, either. I could see by his expression that he was thinking along the same lines as me. They even mocked him with their attempt at witty banter; he told one of the prisoners, who had just lit a cigarette, to stub it out. The prisoner defiantly asked the other officer, "Can we smoke Boss?" The officer said that it was okay, so they all laughed at the Asian officer. He must have been new to the job, and just as naive as I was. He would be learning the hard way, as I would be, but we were both going down very different paths.

As the van drew closer to the courts, a great feeling of sadness came over me as I caught sight of my mother through one of the windows, trying to cross the road towards the courts. Once inside the basement of the courtroom, the handcuffs were removed and we were locked in cells which are always situated below the courtrooms, this is where the phrase 'being sent down' comes from. Court sessions were lengthy and boring. They usually started at around 10.00am and finished at around 4.30pm. Whether you're due in court at 10.00am, 2.00pm, or 4.00pm, you're stuck in those cells all day, which drags on even longer when listening to the grinding banter amongst the 'short termers' such as the burglars and the thieves, continually jabbering about what short sentences they were expecting. They would painfully repeat how they'd be home in time for Christmas and how they can do their 'bird' (sentence) 'standing on their heads'. Their voices would grind on me like that gnawing sensation of a dentist's drill. Each one excitedly chattered away without pausing for a single breath, feeling absolutely no remorse for their crimes or victims, or any thought for those sat in the same cell, facing years of incarceration. The hours dragged on so much that I found myself reading and re-reading all the graffiti scribbled around the cell walls and ceilings, by those who had gone before me, years before. I kept listening out for the clanking of the guard's keys hoping that it was my turn in the dock, or meal time, or anything that will break the painful monotony and get me away from the others' excruciatingly painful rhetoric. I couldn't understand how they were able to talk so easily about everything with a sort of skip in their step and get a buzz from the whole experience. Wasn't being arrested and placed on trial supposed to be painful experience?

It worked on me, but for the others, it was merely a game. I was feeling desperately sad and my stomach was knotted up with anxiety. I didn't want to speak to anyone about anything, all I really wanted right then, was some peace and quiet.

The day dragged on and on until, eventually, it was my turn to make an appearance in the dock. The charges were read out and the prosecuting solicitor, who hadn't done his homework, told the court that I had previous convictions, which wasn't true. Although my solicitor discredited this, and tried his best to put my case to the court emphasising that I was a first time offender, it wasn't enough to get me bail. The Magistrate remanded me in custody for three weeks until my next court appearance. As I was led down the stony steps, back to the cells below, I looked up, towards my mother who was sitting in the gallery above. I could see the hurt on her face; she looked so unhappy. I was devastated. Many, who choose to offend, don't take into account how much it hurts others. It's not just the victims of the crimes who suffer; it's also their families and the offender's family. I was powerless to help my mother, I was so depressed.

After the court sessions had finished, I was taken in the van to Thorpe Arch Remand Centre, (now Wealstun category 'C' closed prison) , near Wetherby. In those days it was for under 21 year olds awaiting trial. En route, we had to stop off at Armley Prison in Leeds, to drop a prisoner off. As we sat staring out of the van windows, we saw a large prison known as a sweat box in the distance. Sweat boxes are the white vans you see with small, square blacked out windows either side. Each window belongs to a small metal cubicle where prisoners were locked inside. They get really hot and are so small, you can barely move, it is an especially tight squeeze when trying to smoke a cigarette. Several tough looking prisoners handcuffed to one another, stepped out of the van. As we looked on, one of the police officers said, "There are your real criminals lads, murderers and rapists - the lot."

I remember how bleak it was in the forecourt of the prison and how I dreaded any thought of ever ending up in such an oppressive looking place. My address was in York, and so, Thorpe Arch Remand Centre was the nearest prison to me. Remand time is a period of major unrest amongst prisoners because of the uncertainty of whether they will be found guilty, how long their sentences will be and when it will actually happen. At least once sentenced, there is a release date which means that they can plan ahead. The type of prison that prisoners are sent to, and the category they become, depends on their crime, their sentence, the risk of harm they are to the public, and how likely they are to try to escape. The first thing that stood out to me in Thorpe Arch, was how much of a 'doddle' it was compared the army glasshouse I'd spent time in two years before. However, it did have other disturbing elements. At first, I was always on edge because I had been expecting to get the same treatment as I'd experienced in the army jail; I'd jump to attention whenever my cell door opened, and was surprised that nobody shouted orders at you. You were allowed to walk instead of march or run, and some of the prisoners even had some friendly banter with the screws (prison officers). The thing that I didn't like, was that there were hundreds of people everywhere and so much going on around me. In the glasshouse, there was only myself and one other prisoner; three at most, at one point. In the reception, we changed into our prison clothes, which were blue denim for convicted prisoners, brown for those on remand and awaiting trial. I was taken by a medical screw to the hospital wing for assessment because I had a history of depression. My cell was at the far end on the right hand side. There were some very disturbed people on the wing. The level of medical knowledge by this medical screw was laughable. He recorded my diagnosis of depression as hypotension, which is abnormally low blood pressure. All I could think, was that if this was a true reflection of the level of medical expertise in prison, then there would be no hope for anyone. My instincts were proved correct many times over the years as I learned first-hand of just how abominable prison medical care was.

It was in Thorpe Arch I first heard the terms 'beast' and 'nonce'. These are names for sex offenders, the word 'nonce' comes from the Latin word 'nonsensical' meaning 'no sense', because sex crimes make no sense. My naivety was my saviour at times though, because while I was on that hospital wing, I was unaware that I was mixing with, and sharing my space with 'nonces'. Once I was transferred to the main wing, I came to realise the enormity of the predicament I had just been in. I felt that something wasn't quite right while I was on the hospital wing; three nights a week, we were escorted by hospital staff in their white coats to the dining hall for the latest movie showing, from a reel to reel projector. Our little group from the hospital wing would always be taken in last where we then ushered on the back row. As we were led through the doors, the whole prison population would be already sat waiting and as we shuffled along the row, everyone would turn their heads to stare at us. This meant absolutely nothing to me at the time, it was later explained to me that it was because some of those with me were sex offenders. Because it was a hospital wing, there was a mixture of medical cases including genuine ones such as epilepsy, depression and physical injuries. Alongside them, were rapists and child molesters. I was horrified when I learned of this, but, the prison grapevine being as it is, they all knew that I was in for violence, so I was safe from accusations.

The main population was more relaxed and I was able to make friends with some lads but there was no atmosphere. I spent a lot of time in the gym as it was a great way to keep my mind and body healthy. There were always those who liked to throw their weight around once they'd developed a bit of muscle, but I had been lifting weights for five years and was already quite muscular. I was lifting heavier weights than most. Male egos really do go wild in prison, but it is a defence mechanism to build on physique in the gym, a place where mutual respect and a lion pack mentality is displayed. Prison is a jungle, and when it comes to the law of the jungle, you have to parade your strengths and hide your weaknesses. A lot of the lads used to train like mad men on the weights, trying to build their size as much as possible, thinking it would make people wary of them. It's a protection thing, so they wouldn't be messed with. You could see a sort of metamorphoses taking place as they grew in size, trying desperately to look tough. I noticed this mostly amongst YP's (Young Prisoners) rather than the older prisoners. This culture was evident during both my 1980's and 1990's sentences.

A major change that I noticed had taken place in the 90's, was that drugs were finding their way into prisons, including steroids, which brought a whole new set of problems. The nature of prison is that everything is magnified and things can seem far worse than they really are. Prisoners overreact at the slightest things, but when drugs are in the mix, things can become even more extreme. All it takes is an innocuous remark, or a rumour to get blown out of proportion and all hell can break loose. The boredom and frustration, brought on by laborious incarceration leads to violence, quite often completely unprovoked. You just have to keep your head down, not allow anyone to intimidate you and do your bird. One day, out of the blue, my father turned up to visit me and burst into tears in the visiting room if they were genuine tears, or tears of self-pity, I will never know.

Three weeks after going into Thorpe Arch, I was bailed at York Magistrates on condition that I resided at South Bank Bail Hostel, near Middlesbrough. My mother was still living in York, so although they'd sent me back to where I originally lived, she was living over 50 miles away.

8. On the run

South Bank Bail Hostel, near Middlesbrough was opposite an old church. I can't remember how many offenders were staying there, but there were about 12 of various ages awaiting their trial dates. I was bored to death there; I was never good at dealing with boredom. Apart from the dreariness of the place, I didn't much like the way it was run, or the other residents' petty ways; there were a few characters in there I couldn't stand to be in the same room with. They all had irritating habits, such as insisting on having their own place at the dinner table, and if anyone sat in their chair they would spit their dummy out, it was pathetic. There was a television room, pool table and a few weights that I used to train with. The gym instructors were okay, this was the only part of the hostel I liked. We had dormitories with about five beds, and there was a curfew at 11.00pm. I used to go and visit my Uncle Billy, who lived nearby on Queen Street, or I would go to the Victoria pub which was practically next door to the hostel. I knew I wouldn't settle at the hostel, from day one, I was restless and anxious. I was worried about what was going to happen at court which made it much harder to settle but eventually, I made the whole situation worse anyway.

One of the other lads, who was a skinhead from Darlington, called John, was also fed up being in there so we started knocking around together. We used to go to the pub and plan how to escape from the hostel. One day, we took a trip to Darlington to do a robbery, the plan was to demand the takings from a rent collector, but he unexpectedly put up a fight, and then, John stabbed him with my knife. We made it back to Middlesbrough on the train and back to the hostel before the curfew. We were at the breakfast table the next

morning when the news on the radio announced that two men were being hunted by police. There were a few knowing glances from the
others, but what we'd done was terrible. One of the 'grasses' (informants) in the hostel reported us to the staff, who called the police. The next day, two detectives from Darlington came to see us and we were questioned at South Bank Police Station. I just wanted this to go away, but I knew that we were in the thick of it and there was no turning back. After what seemed like endless questioning, when we were back at the hostel, John and I both decided to go on the run. We had a mad idea about hitch hiking to London, which we thought was paved with gold. On the day we decided to break out, we cut the alarm wires which were upstairs in one of the dormitories, so when it was time to make our escape, we could make our getaway smoothly and quietly. When night fell, we sneaked out of the top window and made our way down the fire exit steps. We headed for Middlesbrough on foot when John had a stupid idea to burgle someone's house. I'd always hated burglars because it's the invasion of someone's home and privacy. I refused to have anything to do with it, so waited outside while he insisted on doing a 'creep' (night time burglary). Shortly after he broke in to a house, I heard a yell from inside the house and as I looked across, all I saw was John leaping down the stairs, followed by the man he'd tried to burgle. We ran like hell to get away and hid in some nearby bushes for hours. Shortly afterwards, a police car started scouring the area and passed us several times. When we decided to make our move, we were stopped within seconds and questioned. It was obvious to the police officer that we matched the description of who they were looking for, so he radioed through to his colleagues. The next thing I knew, a police van came screeching around the corner to take us away to Middlesbrough Police Station. As we were arrested and led to the rear of the van, one of the more Neanderthal type officers said, "Get in c--t."

Just after being taken in to custody, John decided to be awkward and not tell the police his name, defiant to the end. We were asked to hand over our belongings, and then we were locked up. The two Darlington detectives who had questioned us at South Bank, turned up the next day and took us back to Darlington Police Station which had the worst cells I'd ever been in, and where I spent the longest time in police custody. At first, John and I were in the same cell, and then we were separated. John was pressuring me to take the blame for the stabbing, but I was only going to admit my part of it. Thankfully, John finally confessed that he used the knife, which made things a lot easier for me. He thought that he could intimidate me into taking the blame so he could avoid getting a lengthy sentence which, as a repeat offender, he would. He thought that because I was a first time offender, I should admit to something I hadn't done and accept a few more years inside. Even his cousin, who was also serving time, tried to get me to do it. John was nagging me on the way to court in the sweat van. I had stuck my neck out, but before I met John, I had started out being charged with one attempted robbery, I was now being charged with two attempted robberies, a wounding charge and a burglary. I didn't think that I should be charged with crimes I hadn't committed. Nevertheless, I was still an accomplice, which was enough for me to be charged for just being there. I had to take it on the chin. After entering our pleas at Darlington Magistrates Court, I was taken to Low Newton Remand Centre in County Durham, and because John was older than me, he was taken to Durham Prison.

9. The 'Newbie'

When someone first goes to prison, they've usually been living a reckless life consisting of drink, drugs, and life in the fast lane, so they sleep for hours a day at first to regain energy, exhausted by their lifestyle. Some are very quiet, especially if it is their first time in prison, then as they recover some energy from days of sleeping, and settling into their new surroundings, they start to find their own sets of friends. The days passed quickly really for me, as long as I didn't keep thinking about my release date. Low Newton was very much like Thorpe Arch, but I preferred Low Newton. The trouble was that I was so naïve; I knew I had to change quickly, or I would never survive. Low Newton had exactly the same routine as Thorpe Arch, but it was local, so I could get more visits.

My mother had now moved back to Middlesbrough after exchanging houses again with the same family as before, so she was living back in the same house in Grangetown. My aunt and uncle would bring my mother over for regular visits. Prisoners were always brought into the visiting room first, after being searched, then once everyone was sat at tables, the visitors were brought in. The room was quite large and there was a small canteen where visitors could go and buy cups of tea, sweets, and biscuits. This was when inmates could enjoy a bit of normality with a few simple luxuries, previously taken for granted. They were allowed to drink from a real cup instead of the usual plastic pint mug, eat a donut and some goodies.

I felt sorry for my mother, especially when she cried in the visiting room at the thought of her son being locked up. Prisoners on remand can have more privileges as they haven't been convicted, and are technically innocent, although they are not always treated that way. They are locked up for long hours and often still treated badly by the screws and staff. Once prisoners are sentenced, privileges are reduced, so while on remand, I made the most of it by getting extra tobacco and sweets brought in by visitors, or sent in by parcels. It was quite exciting when the cell door was opened and a screw said to go and sign for a parcel someone had sent. While I was living in York, I befriended a gay couple who ran a local shop close to us in Tang Hall. I was touched when they sent me a parcel containing a huge bar of *Dairy Milk* for Christmas.

We were all in single cells which measured nine feet by five feet, like the other cells I had resided in. It had a single bed, a cork board on the wall, and there was a blue table and chair, where I ate my meals. Heat radiated from large heavy steel pipes situated underneath the barred windows that passed through everyone's cells. They were useful for drying underwear and socks on, and also for passing items to one another through the three inch wide gap in the wall around the pipe. The lad in the next cell was a joker, as were his mates, who I had spent the day with in the holding cells at court before being shipped to Low Newton. Being a new lad or 'newbie' as they say today, I was an easy target. Someone shouted through the gap, "Do you want a 'tab'?" (Cigarette). The most commonly used cigarettes in prison were roll-ups made from cigarette papers and tobacco. Thinking it was a nice gesture, I said, "Yeah, thanks!"
The thinly rolled cigarette was passed along the pipes through the gap from two cells down and as I lit the end of the cigarette, it ignited like a fire cracker burning my lips. I heard hysterical laughter coming from him and his mate next door. The idiot had crushed match heads and put it inside the cigarette paper so that when I lit it, it would burn my mouth. It was this level of immaturity and stupidity from certain individuals that dragged my time out even more. I could cope with being locked up, but not the idiots around me.

Not long after that, I was moved to another cell where I was sharing with someone. I started to talk to him about escaping. When I went on exercise, I would check out the high, barbed wire fences, and the grounds trying to determine how difficult it would be to break out. There were also Alsatians to consider, who would tear me apart if they got me. It was rumoured, that a large hole could be smashed through the fences if something heavy enough was thrown at them. I decided to take my chances, and do it the old fashioned way. I got a metal tin lid from the cleaner's cupboard, which I bent until it was sharp. I began chipping away around the bricks which was surprisingly easy, I would cover it up with paste each night before resuming digging the next night. I didn't get far because my cellmate, who was taken to court one day grassed on me. He must have known that he was going to get bail. The next thing I knew, two screws came into my cell and went straight to the area where I'd been digging. Before I knew it, I was sat in solitary confinement, a bare cell where you have no possessions. When I went in front of the Governor to discover your fate, two screws stood at either side of the desk, but close enough to me that I could feel their breath. This was to protect the Governor from me, in case I attacked him.

He was a slight, balding man with rimmed glasses. He asked me why I had tried to escape.

"I was scared of being raped Sir."

This was something that was stuck in my mind from months before I was sent to prison. I had watched a very disturbing scene from the classic film, *Scum* where a young lad was gang raped. My co-accused, John, had also said that when I got to Durham Prison, I could be raped. That was just him trying to scare me because I'd refused to take the rap for the stabbing. He even told me that Durham Prison was overrun with rats. I asked the screw, who was handcuffed to me on the journey from court to Durham after we were sentenced, if this was true, he replied, "Only the two legged kind."

John's attempt to scare me worked though the fear of being raped was enough for me to try and break out of Low Newton. The Governor looked up at me and said, "I don't think you'll find that will happen."

He then gave me, three days in solitary confinement and two weeks in the block over Christmas, as well as no privileges for two weeks.

Whereas solitary is a single bare cell, the block is a segregated wing consisting of several prisoners. In solitary, I was allowed my mattress after 8.30pm, and every morning I had to take it out and lean it against the wall outside my cell until night. This is just an added punishment so prisoners can't stay in bed all day. This rule was abolished during my next stint in solitary in 1997 when Europe outlawed it.

In the block, prisoners are allowed some of their belongings such as books, writing materials and it's not as harsh as solitary, but the boredom is still horrendous. The block keeps prisoners segregated from the main population, and deprived of privileges such as association (socialising period), and visitation. In another part of the prison, was a grim looking, stone building, known as the 'psycho cell' that one of the cleaners had shown me, and it was used for the most disturbed and violent offenders. It had steps leading up outside of it right to the top. Out of curiosity, I climbed them and looked down through a thick glass roof into what I can only describe as the grimmest dungeon you could imagine. Inside, was a stone slab for a mattress and the walls were cold, thick, solid stone.

Although visits were stopped while I was in the block, the Governor took pity on me, and allowed me a visit from my mother, close to Christmas. She turned up with some presents for me, but had them handed back to her; "Sorry, he's been a naughty boy," one of the screws said to her.
I could see the embarrassment and sadness on her face as he passed my gifts back to her. I was gutted that I had caused her all this grief, but she held on to my presents until I was released. I would go back to my cell after every visit feeling wrecked inside.

Emotions were high at Christmas time in prison. There was a fight in the dinner queue one day and as one of the screws intervened, he said, "Come on now, it's Christmas." We all thought that this was ironically amusing. Visits were more strained than the rest of year too, everyone felt they were missing out on all the festivities and if they had children, they suffered even more.

I thought more about family and friends, and all the celebrations I was missing out on, although, once in prison, you found out who your real friends were. A lot of so called friends forgot about me, or made excuses, and empty promises. Some decided to have nothing to do with me anymore. In prison, there was a term known as, 'prison talk' which means, empty promises from other prisoners who would promise to keep in touch and meet with one another when they were released, but once they had tasted freedom, they disappeared. Only the lifers that I became friends with stayed in contact, as well as one or two others.

On January 19th 1984, I was in the dock at Teesside Crown Court for sentencing with my co-accused, John, standing before Judge Angus Stroyne. There wasn't a jury because we were pleading guilty. A jury is only necessary if defendants plead their innocence, in which case, a jury of 12 people will decide their fate. It seemed an eternity listening to all the legal jargon from the men and women wearing black gowns and horse hair wigs. Some prisoners were very knowledgeable about legal terminology, court procedures and how the legal system worked, and were very interested in it all.

I was sentenced to 30 months Youth Custody, and John got six years imprisonment. I glanced at John as his sentence was handed out. The emotion in his face said it all, he went pale; he hadn't been expecting to get that long and he'd wanted me to take the rap for him. We were both sent to Durham Prison, John was later transferred to Frankland, Category A prison. I later heard he had slashed another prisoner with a broken jam jar.

10. Key to the Door

Whereas 18 is considered the age of maturity these days, it used to be 21 when you came of age in Britain. As an adult, you were considered free to come and go as you pleased, rather than according to your parents' wishes; you were now entitled to 'the key of the door'. In my case, I went into prison a 20 year old boy and left a 21 year old man after I was given the key to freedom by way of parole licence.

Durham Prison is one of the most famous old penal institutions in the United Kingdom. It has been the home of some of Britain's most infamous criminals over the years, including Rose West, Myra Hindley, the Kray twins, Frankie Fraser, and John McVicar. It was also the resting place of a number of men and women executed and buried in its grounds. I was fascinated by the prison's past and by some of its former inmates such, as bank robber, turned journalist and author, John McVicar, who escaped from Durham Prison in 1968. He later published his autobiography, *McVicar by himself*, in 1979, which I was keen to get a copy of. Reading became an important pastime in prison; it helped to pass the torturous hours and often, incarceration makes a prisoner turn to expanding their literary skills. I was reading a book a day, on average.

Although he wasn't in Durham, I was also fascinated by the infamous Glaswegian gangster, turned artist and sculpter, Jimmy Boyle; his story was similar to McVicar's. Boyle published his autobiography *A sense of freedom* in 1977. Both books had a positive influence on my life; albeit not until years after I had first turned the pages. McVicar's autobiography was banned by the

prison authorities and if anyone was caught with the book, it was confiscated. It was
said that this was because, apart from his infamous escape from Durham's E wing in 1968, which was an embarrassment for them, he slags off the prison and the screws, many of whom were still working there when I was in Durham.

My first ever job in Durham was working as a cleaner in the 'search tank', where prisoners were frisked before going to reception. This job was easy, just doing a bit of sweeping and polishing for a few hours a day. The screw in charge of me, Mr. Best, remembered McVicar. This particular screw had a reputation of being a nasty piece of work, but he was alright with me. He told me that McVicar was a real handful, but very intelligent. Someone managed to smuggle McVicar's book in to me by tearing off the front page so it wasn't easily recognisable. However, when one of the screws saw it, the book was removed and kept in my property for when I was released. It mysteriously vanished though when that day arrived. It didn't really matter much; I had read it by then and was inspired by McVicar's educational achievements during his time in prison. It made me want to do the same, so when I was released in 1985, I tried to follow his example.

I was dreading my 30 months ahead, while others just took it as an occupational hazard, all eager to get on the wing to see their buddies. After being processed, signing for our property, getting a bath, and exchanging our clothes for our new prison attire, we were taken to our cells. My new clothes consisted of two blue tee-shirts, a green denim jacket, two blue and white striped shirts, an ill-fitting pair of half-mast blue denims, three pairs of socks, underwear and a pair of hard black shoes that had been worn by hundreds before me and would give you blisters, or cripple your feet. YP's all wore green denim jackets, and the over 21 year olds, known as 'cons', wore blue denim jackets. We weren't allowed to mingle with the 'cons' so our different coloured jackets were to distinguish us from them. YP's all lived on the same landing, and went to work, the gym and showered together. We were given a plastic mug, cutlery, a tooth brush, tooth powder, some White Windsor soap, two towels, two blankets, two pillow cases and two sheets. By the time we were processed and taken to our cells, it was quite late because we had spent all day at court, so by the time we'd gone through the prison reception ordeal, the day was over. Once we were on D Wing, we were allowed a free reception letter and some money to buy a few items or toiletries. We were also entitled to a reception visit which was an extra visit we could request, so friends or family could come and see us as soon as they could get there. In the tuck shop, in the old gallows, I bought half an ounce of Golden Virginia tobacco, a box of matches, some cigarette papers and a penny chew. We were then led up the steep metal stairs to the second landing, called 'the two's,' where the first man was shown to his cell. Soon, we were on the third landing, 'the three's,' where my cell was. Reality hit me as my door was unlocked and I stared into a tiny, cold, dark room; my new home. The sound of the door slamming shut behind me echoed across the whole landing.

There was a single, blue metal hospital style bed, with a striped mattress and a single pillow. I threw all of my bedding on to it and absorbed my new surroundings. In one corner, there was a blue, triangular table, and another smaller table next to it to eat at. The cell window was so high up that I couldn't reach, but when I was alone with my thoughts, I would sit on my wooden chair and gaze up towards the window at the stars which made me wish that I could stand outside in the cold night air.

There was a single light bulb, which I couldn't turn on because the switch was on the other side of the door. At 10:00 pm (lights out), I was plunged into total darkness. Alone in the dark with only my thoughts replaying like a video, my mind drifted back over the day's events which now seemed to be a distant memory. It was difficult to fall asleep and every so often, I would hear the spy hole cover move as a screw took a peek at me, making sure all was well. Thinking of my family, I felt a deep sadness grow inside me. They were so far away and I would not be close to them for quite a while. I started to realise that I would not be able to spend quality time with my mother, or have her home cooking to look forward to for a long time.

I thought about how she was alone in her house in Middlesbrough. She told me years later, that just after I was sentenced, she went to a cafe and bought a coffee which lasted an hour; she'd just sat there, numb with shock, staring into space. She couldn't believe that her son, who had always been such a good kid in the past, was in now one of the most notorious prisons in the country.

I must have drifted off to sleep, because suddenly, I was woken by a bright light in my face as the screws stomped along the landings, switching lights on and peering through our spy holes. It was morning and time to get up. It was a cold winter's day and as I forced myself out of bed and stood on to the icy cold floor, I could hear loud, piercing echoes of screws shouting to one another:
"All ready on the two's, Mr. Pendlworth?"
"All ready on the two's, Sir." came the response.
"All ready on three's, Mr Stevens?"
"All ready on three's, Sir."
Then the order followed, "Okay unlock!"

The doors were unlocked and opened slightly. I popped my head out where I could see lines of men wearing blue tee shirts and blue denims, sleepily dragging themselves along the landing. It was 6:30am. I could see that they were all carrying plastic chamber pots to slop out their overnight waste. In their other hands, were bowls to collect water to wash their hands and faces in, and white plastic jugs to collect drinking water.

In those days, we didn't have toilets and washbasins in the cells, so we had to go to the toilet in plastic chamber pots. Three times a day, we were unlocked to dispose of it all in a daily ritual known as 'slopping out', where we emptied our pots into large sinks in a recess area at the foot of each landing. Tempers were frayed, as it was far too early in the morning to be suddenly woken by a bright light and a bang on the door, followed by a screw bellowing, "slop out!"
There was one toilet in the recess area and if you could get there before someone else beat you to it, you made the most of it. I never thought that using a toilet could be such a luxury, but it was at times like that when I realised just how much I had taken everything in life

for granted. The disadvantage of the toilet though, was that the cubicle door was only waist high, so while everyone was crammed in the packed recess area slopping out, they could see the person in front sitting on the toilet. We were all used to not having any kind of privacy though, because we had to do our business in the cells, there was a mutual respect amongst us. We always gave one another as much privacy as possible. When I had to squat over my pot in the cell, my cellmate would read a newspaper or if he was lying on his bed, he would turn to face the wall. We didn't have toilets in those days because Durham dated from the Victorian era and wasn't originally designed to have them.

Some of the prisoners, who couldn't stomach the stench of their waste festering at the foot of their bed would try and persuade a screw to let them use the toilet in the recess area. Some power mad screws wouldn't allow it, so they used to do their business on a newspaper, fold it up like a parcel (a shit parcel) and throw it through the bars. I would often see one drop past my window from the cells above. In the morning, some other poor mug would end up having to scoop it up. If someone had bad guts and desperately needed to go, they would plead with the screws to let them use the recess toilet. There were some who were okay and would allow them to use it, and some who just wouldn't. Sometimes, when coming back from work, or a visit, I would see rows of fallen 'tallies' (metal number plates) when prisoners had pressed their buzzers to get the screws attention who were standing at one end of the landing, ignoring them all.

As the morning ritual unfolded, once we had collected our water and slopped out, a screw would come to each cell with a wooden box containing our individually named razor blades. The razor blades were wrapped in paper with our names on, to make sure we got the right one because we used the same blade every morning for that week. We always had to be clean shaven unless we made a formal application, and were granted permission to grow facial hair as it was classed as changing our appearance. Once we had had time to shave, our razors were collected back, but while we were waiting for them to be collected, we used this period to quickly slice our matches into four so they would last longer. It required skill to do this, and make sure that the sulphur remained intact. As my first eventful day in Durham continued, to my relief, I saw some familiar faces from Low Newton. There was one lad, who we nicknamed 'Elvis'. I had shared a cell with him in Low Newton. He was now banged up on the same landing and there were a couple of others I recognised, who all looked as though reality was just kicking in for them too.

As I walked down the flights of metal stairs for breakfast, my attention was suddenly caught by what looked like a female prisoner strutting along the landing like a model on a catwalk. He had a certain rapport with the screws and other prisoners; all I could hear were shouts of, "Lesley, Lesley!" echoing from all directions. Lesley was the first transgender person I had ever seen, and from what I was seeing, and hearing, she was a very popular prisoner. She was going through a sex change using hormone medication and living as a woman. I could see that she loved the attention she received, as much as everyone enjoyed having such a great character around to brighten up the long, dismal days. Once a week, we all congregated outside the communal shower block. Lesley had to have a bath and was segregated from the rest of us. I was told it was because of her body changes and that she would get excited being around us but as I have said, prison gossip is even worse than gossip on the outside. Lesley was always in and out of prison for soliciting in Newcastle's West End on a regular basis. She hadn't been released for long, when one day, while gazing through my cell window, I saw a screw escorting her back in again. Someone yelled from their cell window, "What you in for Lesley?"
"Murder!" she replied.

She was charged for murdering her father having stabbed him with a potato peeler, but was eventually acquitted. She was a regular face in the prison and it would have been difficult to distinguish her from any other woman, had we not known who she was. Every Sunday morning, the Chapel was packed with prisoners wanting a glimpse of Lesley who basked in all the attention she was getting. I very much doubt that they were all in Chapel because they had all suddenly seen the light. It was just an extra hour out of our cells. The night before being released, I waved across to Lesley's cell to say goodbye and she waved back. Years later, I heard that Lesley had died from AIDS in Newcastle.

Those who didn't have a job were locked up for 23 hours a day, the only break from the endless monotony of bang-up was exercise. Around 11.00am each morning, a screw would shout, "Exercise! Press your buzzers if you want to go on exercise!!"
Exercise was a daily ritual when we were given an hour to stretch our legs and meet one another. We would walk around in circles, around the perimeter of the exercise yard, we weren't allowed to mingle in numbers more than three, walk anti-clockwise, or stop walking.

One day, while we were all congregated at the entrance to the exercise yard, a child abuser from the VP (Vulnerable Prisoner) wing had rang his bell and asked one of the screws if he could come on exercise with the rest of us. The screw strongly advised against it as it could only cause trouble but the prisoner was persistent in demonstrating that it was his 'right'. A very reluctant prison officer unlocked his cell door and allowed him to come out on the yard with the rest of us. As he joined the crowd at the entrance, I could see him being pushed and shoved, while one or two gave him a dig. Once we were in the yard, everyone started taunting him, so he started throwing stones and shouting obscenities at us. The screws could see a potential riot brewing and took him back to his cell.

Prison isn't just for a particular type of person, as one might expect. Prisoners come in all shapes and sizes, nationalities, ages and backgrounds. There were murderers, shop lifters, rapists, television licence dodgers and some, who preferred spending six weeks a year in prison, rather than paying child maintenance. It was a real mixed bag of people. The prison was full of characters, some of who scared me and fascinated me at the same time.

There was one ruthless well-known criminal called Freddie Mills (Fred the Head), who was very loud, and as large as life. He was allowed to walk around as he pleased and the screws never challenged him. He would go berserk at night hammering on his cell door, releasing his pent up anger, but was never nicked for it. Four armed robbers came in once, having just received 12 years each for a well-executed heist on a security van. They had stolen £95,000, which hadn't been recovered; it was buried beneath the ground somewhere, they decided to send a relative to dig it up. Unfortunately for them, the police were waiting and recovered the lot. The digger got 18 months while the others now had a long stretch ahead of them for nothing.

As I got to the breakfast queue, a hugely built prisoner who was as 'camp' as they come, was eyeing up the new batch of young prisoners. He was in charge of the cleaners who also served food to prisoners alongside some of the screws.

The eldest character, was old Albert, who had spent his lifetime in and out of Durham since his first sentence in the 1950's when he was sentenced to seven years for stealing a shirt from a shop. He was about 72 and would always run up to me and walk alongside me chattering away. I would see him every day scurrying along D Wing, picking up dog ends from the floor until he had enough to make a new cigarette. A lot of the prisoners did the same. Albert was respected by the screws due to his age, the fact he was harmless and because they had all known him for so long. He eventually died in the prison, which may sound sad, but he was amongst people he regarded as family.

To some prisoners, prison was home. There was a well-known tramp who would deliberately get himself sent back to prison by smashing a window, or stealing something as soon as he was released. He saw the prison as his home, which was better than his living conditions on the streets. Towards Christmas, a lot of homeless people would do the same. Tragically, some prisoners preferred to be in prison, rather than in their alternative living arrangements. It wasn't necessarily because they couldn't face responsibility or were hopeless cases or even persistent offenders as many would think. In many cases, it was because of mental illness or an inability to cope with the outside world. Then there were those who lived hand to mouth on the nearby streets, who merely wanted to be inside during the cold winter months, Durham Prison was a welcome alternative. For others, prison life was better than their abusive, violent and dysfunctional home lives. This doesn't mean that prison was easy, just that their home lives were worse than prison life. I remember one of the Governors at Wealstun Prison telling me that one elderly prisoner, who also died in prison, had named him as his next of kin as he didn't have any family.

As we shuffled along the queue for our breakfast, we picked up a metal silver tray which had different sections. It had a circular one for a mug, another partition for cutlery, then two square sections for the main course and for pudding (duff). There were several long tables where a line of inmate cleaners and screws, wearing white coats stood slopping food from huge pans on to the prisoners' trays. We got two dollops of porridge that was thick enough to cement the cracks in the cell walls. We got a scoop of sugar, that I used to save in a jar so I could add extra sugar to my cereal. We got a boiled egg with four slices of bread and a round knob of butter. At the end of the line, were two large urns, one was coffee, and the other, tea. Meals were the highlight of our day. Lunch would be something like chicken or vegetable pie, mash and gravy with a sponge and custard duff. At tea time, around 4:30 pm, it was a lighter meal, sometimes with chips and ham and a different piece of fruit each day. At weekends we used to get large homemade biscuits, which were delicious. Each night, around 9:00pm when we were all locked in for the night, a screw and a kitchen orderly would visit the cells with a tea urn perched on top of a trolley and a tray of left over biscuits. During the day, once we'd all taken our food to our cells, we were locked in. After lunch, the cells were unlocked so we could put our trays outside the cell, on the floor for the cleaners to collect. The whole prison would then turn silent for about an hour and a half while everyone took 40 winks. Sometimes, you could hear a pin drop, apart from the distant sounds of soft music from transistor radios around the prison. At about 2:00 pm, doors were unlocked for those who had to go back to work, and for those whose relatives or friends had come to visit them.

One thing about prison life which has never changed is that prisoners cannot handle change. It can be the smallest thing from meals being served late, mail not being given out at the usual time, or prisoners' cells not being unlocked at their usual time. This can create much disruption because prisoners live by daily routine and structure. I have seen trouble brew over things such as the menu being changed. All it takes is the slightest alteration and a full scale fight could break out. I still thrive on routine which probably comes from my childhood, which was built on routine, and also through spending part of my life in various institutions. When I was at University, I would struggle with the three months summer break because it meant my routine had been broken. I felt as lost as I had when I was first released from prison.

Durham Prison was infested with cockroaches, due to lack of proper sanitation. The building was over 170 years old and had housed prisoners for many decades. We ate in our cells, amongst the cockroaches and human waste. I was on the top bunk so my head was near the air vent, where the cockroaches crawled through. I blocked all the holes but they still crawled underneath the cell door. Sometimes, I would move a towel or a book and find one underneath it. Sometimes they appeared in food; I remember seeing a long antennae poking out of my mash one day, and another time I ate half a cockroach, thinking it was just a burnt chip.

Everything echoed loudly through the prison, slamming gates and cell doors resonated across the whole building. When I was in my cell I could hear the screws' boots squeak as they stomped along the metal landings. During visiting hours I would listen out carefully, hoping their footsteps would get closer and that I would be unlocked because I had a visitor. The steps would get louder and there would be a brief pause outside as the screw checked my identity card, then the sound of the keys turning in the keyhole. We all had identity cards outside the cell in a wooden slot. They displayed our name, prison number, sentence, dietary requirements, and were different colours according to our religion; white for Protestants and red for Catholics.

Every evening, we were unlocked for association which was for socialising, between 6:00pm to 8.30pm. We could leave our cell doors open, mingle with one another, play pool, and watch television. Once we were banged up for the night, we would read books from the prison library, study, write letters and listen to our radios. Once a week our laundry was changed, we got fresh linen from the cleaners and then we would all congregate at the huge communal shower room, hand over our dirty clothes to a screw on reception in exchange for fresh clothing, which was placed in a basket to collect after we'd finished showering.

I had several different cells during my time in Durham, my first being a single on A Wing; A3 was the YP wing. My first cell was like an ice box. I sat in it all day with a blanket wrapped around me. From my window, I could see the women's E Wing situated on H Block, where McVicar escaped in 1968. The women used to play their music loud enough for us to hear and they would wave across and shout to us. I remember one day, hearing the dulcet tones of Bob Marley coming from one of their cell windows filling the air, and for a short time, the music took us beyond the prison walls.

Several weeks later, I was moved to another cell where I had a cellmate called Jonesy who loved himself. He made my life a misery, so I requested a cell change. One day in the gym, Jonesy was taunting me in front of his mates, so I squared up to him but he backed down and left me alone after that.

After working in the search tank, I had another job, sewing mail bags in the workshops at the rate of two pence a bag. Those who didn't work, were given an allowance of £1.13 per week. As well as the machinists and hand stitchers sewing mailbags for Royal Mail, some of the others produced goal nets for football clubs and camouflage nets for the army. I wasn't interested in this work at all. I sat and did nothing. The workplace was run by the only female screw in the prison, who made some of the men look like pussy cats. She sat, perched high on a chair at the head of the room overlooking four rows of prisoners working away, earning their pittance of pay. One day, she had me escorted back to my cell after noticing I hadn't attempted to sew a single stitch. She unknowingly did me a great favour because I was placed on educational classes after that. I also got my wish to be moved to another cell, which was situated close to the old gallows callously referred to by the screws as the 'topping shed'.

Durham was one of the few prisons to retain a permanent gallows housed at the end of D Wing which was built in 1925. It had two condemned cells, one adjacent to the gallows and one separated from the execution chamber by a corridor that led to the exercise yard. The main condemned cell was formed from three standard cells knocked into one and had a toilet and washbasin. There was a small lobby between the cell and the gallows room.

There was a mortuary in the yard adjoining the ground floor of the execution chamber. Parts of the execution block still remain to this day, although the condemned cell has been removed and the pit covered over. This area is now used for storage. When I queued at the tuck shop to buy my tobacco, I could see the old trap door on the ceiling above. Next to the old trap, on the other side, was a steel pedal the screw used to keep his foot on it to prevent the trap doors from opening, should there be a last minute reprieve for the condemned prisoner. From my cell, I could see directly into the cell where prisoners had spent their final night before execution which was above the tuck shop. The inside of the cell was still there, but what used to be the door, was now bricked up.

In the early 1990's when the prison was being modernised, graves of some of the executed were disturbed, including that of Mary Ann Cotton. A pair of shoes belonging to her were found along with her bones. Several bodies, including Cotton's, were removed and were later cremated. All of the inmates hanged in the 20th Century were buried alongside the prison hospital wall with only a broad arrow and the date of execution carved into the wall to mark the location of their grave. The original instructions, regarding the burial of executed inmates, stated that the only clothing an inmate should be buried in was a prison issue shirt. The body was to be placed into a pine box, covered with quicklime and holes were to be bored into the box before burial. During my time there, there were many accounts of paranormal activity which scared people senseless, myself included. Given the prison's sinister history then, it would seem rather silly to tamper with the unknown but boredom is a big problem in prison. I felt I had to try and alleviate boredom somehow. One night, my cellmate, Tim and I decided to make our own Ouija board. Tim had a lot of experience with this sort of thing but it was a stupid idea which turned into a terrifying ordeal. It started with tables shaking, we heard screams and disembodied voices from inside the cell, and objects such as our chamber pots toppled over. The three sleepless nights that followed were the longest that I remember, but luckily, we didn't feel the need to tell the screws what we had done. I didn't touch a Ouija board again until I started joining in organised ghost hunts over 28 years later. I have always had an interest in the paranormal but firmly believe that things I don't understand, should be left well alone.

We had a Scottish screw in charge of us called Mr Assenti, who had a firm, but fair attitude. There were some screws who just wanted to make the prisoners' lives a misery but I tried to avoid them as much as possible. Mr Assenti was typical old school; a former army Sergeant Major. He was short in stature and when he walked, his back was ramrod straight, proudly displaying his medal ribbons on his tunic. He was in charge of all the YP's, and although he was strict, he was respected by us all. After two weeks of sewing mailbags, my brain was so numb; I just wanted a different job, so I asked one of the nicer screws, Mr Coates, if he could help. A few days later, a small slip of paper was slid underneath my cell door telling me that I was to attend educational classes the next day. This would encourage me to knuckle down and study, as McVicar's book had inspired me to do, but it would be many years later before I actually made some real educational achievements. Classes consisted of basic learning skills to accredited qualifications. During that summer, I was shipped out to Castington Young Offenders' Institute in Northumberland, next to Acklington's Category C Adult prison. I detested it. A lot of the other YP's acted like children. I think my short stint in the army helped me grow up a bit, because I always seemed to have an older head than a lot of the others. Then again, a lot of the other prisoners were several years younger than me, and I would soon be too old to be in there anyway. It was just a month before my 21st birthday, after which, I couldn't be held in a Young Offenders' Institution and would be returned to Durham. During my stay, fires were lit every night and cells were smashed up. It was a world away from Durham, yet even with its downsides, it was where I preferred to be with the more mature convicts.

Prisoners in Young Offender Institutions lack any form of maturity, so violence is even more spontaneous. YP's are entering adulthood and want to prove themselves, so bullying was more rife amongst the youngest prisoners who wanted to gain fearsome reputations.

In Castington, we had toilets and washbasins in our cells, a nice dining hall to sit and eat our meals in and jobs to go to, despite this, I just couldn't stand the place. I wanted to get out of there as soon as possible. On the positive side of things, they had an excellent gym and we were allowed to run laps around the inside perimeter.

It was a stifling summer in 1984, one of the hottest summers I can remember. The heat from the sun would sometimes beam through the cell windows, but we weren't allowed to hang a cover or blanket up to block out the sunlight. I developed a terrible migraine. It felt as though someone was sticking a sharp object through my eye socket. The pain was excruciating but I couldn't leave the cell or hide from the direct rays of the sun. I became so ill that I started vomiting. Then, one Sunday, unable to suffer the pain anymore, I rang the bell and requested to see the doctor. I was warned that if the doctor had to make a special journey to come out see me, I'd be confined to my cell for three days because to come out on a Sunday was an inconvenience for him, I was in too much pain to care. When the doctor eventually turned up, he prescribed me a few aspirin and had me sent back to my cell. I was then punished for being unwell and causing such an inconvenience but it was normal to be treated with such contempt by the prison's medical staff. The mentality of these fools was to confine me to my cell for three days, where I was in constant pain from the direct sunlight for even longer periods of time. At least before then, I could go to the dining hall for my meals to escape the heat for a short time, whereas now I was having all my meals brought to my cell.

Prison medical care for inmates was diabolical. Rude, uncaring people ran the prison's medical centre, I despised the medical staff. If a prisoner was on medication, it was slammed down in front of them when they went to collect it. I could see the hatred in their faces as they spoke down to us. Prisoners were given aspirin water for every type of ailment, even some of most serious injuries. I once remember a prisoner being given aspirin water after breaking his arm. Aspirin water was one or two aspirins crushed into water, and the answer to everything. During my second time in prison, some of my gums became infected causing toothache, but prison health care was so bad that my teeth were left to rot. When I was released, I had to have several removed.

One the nicer screws, Mr O'Brien, was on duty most of the time and we struck up a good rapport. He was from my neck of the woods in Eston and years later, I would see him in Eston Labour Club at weekends, when we would have a catch up. Once I turned 21, I was finally transferred from Castington back to Durham. Shortly after getting back, I got a job in the kitchen which is one of the most popular jobs in any prison.

The kitchen, like the rest of the prison had a cockroach infestation. Once when I moved a bag of flour, hoards of them ran from underneath and across the kitchen floor. Working in the kitchen had certain privileges, such as extra portions of food, more than one shower a week, and more changes of clothing. We wore white tee shirts instead of the usual blue ones and the kitchen screws wore white coats. Like in most prisons, the screws who worked with prisoners developed better relationships with prisoners, compared to those who only worked on the landings. The work screws treated their prisoner sidekicks like workmates, developing a rapport and mutual respect.

Several months earlier, I had applied for parole consideration, we prisoners, called this 'jam roll'. Parole is when a prisoner serves the remainder of their sentence released back into the community. It involves regular meetings with a probation officer who makes sure they are complying with the conditions of their parole and settling back into their lives. If they are violating their parole conditions or not adjusting to life outside prison, they can be recalled to complete their sentence in prison.

The day I got my answer, I was lying on my bed. I could hear several prisoners talking outside on the landing, waiting to be let into their cells. It was about 4:00pm and the lads had just finished work. When prisoners returned from work or a visit, a screw escorted them back to the landing to wait to be let in. If there were no screws around, one of us would have to go to the office and ask to be let in. I didn't like doing this because the screws office was a place of hostility. In the office, there were usually a half a dozen screws sitting around doing nothing. It felt quite intimidating at times, as they would glare at you whenever you entered. The wing officer, a principle officer (PO) on D Wing, was unapproachable and always looked as though on the verge of a nervous breakdown. He used to sit at his desk with his bright red face looking ready to explode any moment. His blood pressure must have been high. A PO was in charge of the wing and the senior officer (SO), was the next rank down.

A sheet of paper slid underneath my door. I recognised it as being from the Home Office from the logo at the top of the page. I knew it was my parole answer, so bracing myself for bad news, I read down the page until I saw the words: 'A panel of the parole board considered your case on 19 August 1984 and found you suitable for release on parole licence from 4 September 1984'

Nowadays, prisoners are summoned to the office to see the PO, who presents them with the paper and discusses their conditions with them. Holding the letter in my hand that listed my conditions and recommended date of release, was all I needed and the feeling inside was one of elation. I had butterflies, adrenaline was pumping and my mind was racing. I had only been in prison for 10 months, but it had seemed like years. It had been my first time in prison for any length of time and the environment was far removed from any kind of reality.

I felt isolated from the outside world; nothing in prison ever gave me a sense of normality. The false environment and community, the different behaviours I'd seen, and what could begin as a small problem would be magnified until it became a very large problem. It made me view things from a different perspective to how I might have seen things on the outside. It soon got around the prison grapevine that my parole had come through. My Liverpudlian mate who I had worked with in the mailbag workshop, called 'Scouse', shouted through my cell door, "I heard you got your parole mate!"

"Yeah." I shouted back.

"Well done, mate"

Each day became longer than usual, because I was urging my release day on as it was only days away. This is referred to as being 'gate happy'.

The day before my release, I was taken to reception to check my property and sign for it. I noticed that McVicar's book had vanished from my property and nobody knew what I was talking about when I asked where it was. At least I could buy my own copy when I was out. Once I had signed for my property ready for the following day's release, I knew my parole hadn't been a mistake or a dream. I was actually on my way home but even though it was official, I couldn't help but think that something could go wrong. I became paranoid, wondering what would happen if someone started trouble with me, jealous that I was going home, wondering if I should stay in my cell for the next few days in case anything happened and my parole got revoked before I was even released. It never happened. I was unlocked early that morning and told to be ready in 10 minutes. They didn't have to hurry me, I'd been ready for hours. I used those 10 minutes to say goodbye to Scouse and some of the others. My release day was an exciting experience, I was on cloud nine. There was no point trying to sleep the night before, I was too excited. I had my breakfast in the reception area that morning while paperwork was being prepared. Everyone made sure they ate their breakfast before being released, even if they were too excited to have any appetite. Superstition says that if you don't eat it, you come back to finish it.

A few of us were being released that morning, one of the lads was arguing with the screw at the desk and was sent back to his cell. This made me panic that the same could happen to me, so I kept me head down and my mouth shut.

We were handed cardboard boxes with our names and numbers on containing the clothes we were wearing when we came to prison. We were then told to go and get changed.

On release, unless they have served a long time, or they have gained or lost a significant amount of weight, prisoners were given the clothes they were wearing when they were first brought to prison. One of the prisoners was a huge black guy, well over six feet tall and of massive build. He was arrested at Christmas wearing a Santa Claus costume, so he had to travel home on a bus dressed as Santa in the middle of a hot summer's day.

After we had changed, we were handed our property, it was nice to be able to hold my wallet and handle money again. It made me feel like a proper person again. We didn't handle money while in prison. We were given a week's social security money and a green form to take to the job centre to sign on for unemployment benefit. The ultimate feeling of excitement was when I was anxiously waiting in line at the gate, listening for my name to be called out by the screw, who read from a list. As each person's name was called out, the screw opened the door for them to step out. When my turn finally came, I stepped out and was immediately hit by the fresh air and smell of flowers. The air seemed different outside compared to the grey, dull, dead air within the prison grounds. Another lad, also from Middlesbrough was released with me, so we tagged along together. I saw the beautiful surroundings of Durham City as we walked towards the train station and soaked in every moment. I couldn't wait to get back to see my mother, who had stood by me. She wrote letters to me as often as possible and every month she had religiously made the long trip to Durham and back to visit me. She bought me my favourite 45 record, *Radio Ga Ga,* by Queen. When I heard it on my radio in prison, I would try to get a good signal so I could hear it through the crackling airwaves.

Once I was back in Middlesbrough, I was given instructions to go and meet my probation officer, Russell Bruce who at the time of writing is now the current Chief Executive of the Durham Tees Valley Probation Trust. He was quite new to his work back in the 1980's and about the same age as me. Each week, I visited him to talk through what I'd been up to, but my euphoria was short lived, as once again, I became restless and bored with my life. I began to turn up for my appointments under the influence of alcohol. I was continually drifting, unsure about what do with my life; I was drinking too much and being erratic. My parole licence was supposed to last for 10 months but Mr Bruce was concerned about me and the safety of others, so he contacted the Home Office. Two weeks later and after only six months of being free, the Home Office recalled me back to prison.

11. Recalled

It happened one night at around 7:30pm while I was getting ready for a night out. There was a knock at the door. When I moved the curtains, I could see a police sergeant and I knew why they'd come. They were unaware of why they had been sent to arrest me, but I knew my parole had been revoked. I was taken back to Durham Prison to complete another pointless four months. I went through the same old rigmarole of reception and this time I was taken to D Wing where I shared a cell with two others. Most of the cells had three men sharing the nine feet by five feet space. I tried to talk to a couple of screws to see if I could appeal, but it was falling on deaf ears. Shortly after being back, I was transferred to C Wing, which was a sort of privileged wing. It had a dartboard, pool table and television room as did the other wings but it had a different ambience altogether. Some of the cons played chess and dominoes. It was smaller compared to the main D Wing landing. Prisoners had to be selected for C Wing. It was where the red band trustees, low risk and short termers were housed. I don't know why I was taken to C Wing, but it was probably because I was only there for four months. Going back to Durham Prison had a bad psychological effect on me; I was stressed with the shock of being recalled.

As part of the reception process, prisoners were taken to the see the Governor the next day, where they would be asked their profession and various other things. Whatever they said that day would determine the sort of jobs they would be allocated. For example, if they had said they had experience in catering, they could get one of the best jobs in the prison as a kitchen orderly.

He told me that they would be releasing me again on licence as soon as possible, as they felt I didn't need to be in there. Naturally this lifted my spirits. My new cell was opposite the main gate, and at night I could hear the pub goers leaving the local boozer. I hated my cellmate and he hated me, but it wasn't long to endure - at least in real time anyway - but in prison, time is not real. It seems like an eternity as one day rolls into the next. I knocked about with some good guys, such as 'Fingers' who, at some point in his life had some of his fingers chopped off. He was a fellow body builder so we used to chat about training and how it gave us a sense of wellbeing. Also, within my close circle of friends was another chap called Andy, who had been the manager of a North East 1980's chart band. A few doors away, was a red band called Steve who was a former soldier in the Army Intelligence Corps. Red bands were trustee prisoners, who had extra privileges and were all housed on C Wing. One of the best jobs in the prison that red bands could do was working in the Officer's Mess. I couldn't get over how different C Wing was and how different the prisoners were compared to the others, but like Castington, this privileged environment also nauseated me. I hated to see grovelling and sucking up. I preferred to be with the majority, where we were all in the same boat. I didn't ask to go on C Wing.

I picked up education classes from where I'd left off and started studying English Language towards my first ever exam. The teachers who worked at the prison were very approachable and easy going, but it was common to get schoolboy crushes on some of them. Having been deprived of female company for so long, it was easy to cling on to anything that touched your heart. It was infatuation and nothing more, but it could bring out the more sensitive side of a man. One of my fellow prisoners had an affair with a teacher and the last I heard, they got married on his release. The interaction between prisoners and teachers made prison life a lot easier. We spent most of our days with them so we developed a good rapport and bond. They made us feel human addressing us informally, sometimes by our first names. This familiarity was disapproved of by some of the screws, who objected to the teachers treating prisoners with such respect. Thankfully, our liberal thinking teachers had their own way of doing things, and it was always nice to have a little victory over the screws. Attending classes was a huge turn around for me going from years of despising education and teachers, to enjoying every minute of it. Prison education was my first encounter with academia since I walked out of my school exams five years earlier.

On the day of the exam I was to wait inside my cell until I was collected and taken to another cell where I would sit my test. Suddenly, my cell door opened when I was greeted by a screw and one of the teachers called Debbie who was also the education officer at the time. I was led to an empty cell on the ones to sit my test. I flew through the questions in the hour I was given, but I still had to wait a while until I was unlocked. Later, I felt as though I'd achieved something for the first time in my life. I went back to my cell and laid down on my bed to reflect. My results arrived after I'd been released from prison and I'd gained an RSA English Language qualification. My mother was very proud that day. She often used to recall when she used to leave the prison after visiting me, how she'd see students sat in their classrooms at Durham University and wished that I was there instead.

Although I was pleased with myself for completing my very first exam, circumstances were about to spoil everything. Three months had passed since the Governor had told me that I would be released on licence again, so I was so chuffed to bits when I was told that I was getting out four weeks early. The day before I was to be released again, I was taken to reception to check my property. This confirmed in my mind that I was going home again. Once you've checked your property, prisoners are taken straight back to their cells, so when I was told that the principle officer wanted to see me, I knew something was wrong. I was told that they had made a mistake and that I wasn't being released after all. He apologised and although I only had four weeks left to serve, it had a bad effect on me. I had built my hopes up. My anxiety levels were so high after that, while I was eating my lunch that afternoon, my nose suddenly started to bleed into my soup. I was fed up with cockroaches in the cell, I didn't get on with my cellmate, and I had just had a nasty shock. I wasn't in the best of moods. It wasn't for long though, there were only weeks left and that thought kept me going.

As the weeks passed, I was getting gate happy again, and then finally, my earliest date of release (EDR) arrived. This is the release date, where the sentence ends permanently. Remission is automatically taken off for good behaviour at the start of a sentence. In my case, a third of my sentence (10 months) was taken off for good behaviour. This meant that I was to serve a total of 20 months, six of which, I served on parole licence and 14 in prison. A prisoner's latest date of release (LDR) is their latest possible release date of their sentence. If a prisoner serving five years loses all of their remission, their LDR will be after they have completed a full five years. I had about an extra 10 days to serve of lost remission. Three days were added to my sentence for throwing part of my table through the bars of my cell window when I was at Castington and seven days were added for my attempted escape. I was lucky because they charged me for damaging the cell wall rather than attempting to escape. Had they charged me for attempting to escape, I could have ended up serving several extra years.

12. Making a Fresh Start

Back home in Middlesbrough, I was leading a stable lifestyle. I was keen on fitness and weight training, going to Eston Sports Hall several times a week and doing long distance running. When I was first released from prison, I was too weak to run. It took several weeks of my mother's cooking to get me back to normal. Not long after, I started getting restless and had some crazy ideas to go travelling around the country. I was always searching for something but never knew what. All I knew, was that I couldn't settle in Teesside. I set off for Birmingham and managed to find a hostel to stay at called *The Boot* in Digbeth. The Boot was for homeless people. It had a reception area leading to a television room and had a dormitory with about 30 beds. As I got to know people, I discovered there was a group of rent boys there and each night they would go and sell their wares to the highest bidder. They were intimidating towards younger residents, who were encouraged to join them. One night, one of them was coerced into having sex with two men in a car. After that, he would wake up in the middle of the night, screaming and crying. One of the rent boys used to meet a Catholic Priest each night outside *The Boot*, they would then go off somewhere else. It was seedy and not the kind of environment I wanted to be in. The staff who ran *The Boot*, were a great bunch of well-meaning people who helped me find somewhere more permanent to live. It was in a place called Hockley, which wasn't far from Handsworth which was notorious for riots and a high crime rate. During my time in Birmingham, I associated with the seedier side of life. One of the lads from the hostel introduced me to his mates at a 24 hour café in Digbeth run by two gay men. Late at night it would be full of transgender men who used it as a late night stop off in between soliciting themselves on the streets. Most nights there would be a fight between some of them over disputes, or just jealousy, because one had got more punters than the other, or had encroached on another's patch.

Every day, I would go to a gay bar called *Legends*. It was full of interesting characters. I can remember it was next to a cinema which at the time was showing *Rocky IV*. I didn't get much sleep in the hostel, and I can recall trying to keep myself awake during day while sitting in *Legends*. Although I wasn't gay, I liked the atmosphere such bars had.

Birmingham was a scary place for me back then and very much a multi-cultural society. This was all new to me. On Teesside, there wasn't a large multi-cultural community, so I found it extremely intimidating. I had heard a lot about race related violence in Birmingham and the racial tensions between minorities and the police. One night in Hockley, outside my bedroom window, a black pimp beat up a prostitute, while in Handsworth on another occasion, someone was blasted with a shotgun in a café. It was a hotbed of criminal activity. During the mid 80's, I was seeing first-hand the effects Britain's high unemployment, oppressiveness, racism and recession was having on different communities in the North East and the Midlands. I had left Teesside, where I witnessed the declining steel industry and all the effects it had on local people and now in Birmingham, I was witnessing racism and violence fuelled by social deprivation and police harassment. I could feel the tension around me like a pressure cooker about to explode. Then in September 1985, riots broke out.

When I moved into my new bedsit in Hockley, I was awarded Housing Benefit from the local council, but as soon as I received the cheque which included four weeks arrears, I cashed it and went on a boozing spree. I knew this would catch up with me eventually, but I rarely thought of consequences. That was exactly my problem. I couldn't cash it at a Post Office because it was addressed to the landlord. I'd met Billy at *The Boot*. He had a lot of contacts, so I asked him if he knew a way to get it cashed. He took me to a very shifty looking café and as we approached, a black man standing outside asked if we wanted to buy some drugs, which we refused. We walked into the café, and I was introduced to the Chinese owner, who examined the cheque and after negotiating his percentage, cashed it for me. Of course, my landlord at the bedsit got wind of my shenanigans and asked me to leave, so I returned to Middlesbrough.

Once I was back home, I tried to lead as much of a normal life as possible, but I was 21 years old with no qualifications thanks to my disastrous schooling; been dishonourably discharged from the army; had a criminal record and a history of clinical depression. There weren't many options open to me at the time. I thought that if I was to find work, I had to focus on jobs where I wouldn't be asked if I had a criminal record. Even so, I was feeling hyper active now and ready to enjoy life and take the bull by the horns. I was super fit and raring to find something to stimulate me. I had spent some time unemployed where I used to sign on at Hadrian House Social Security building in Eston once a fortnight. In the meantime, I was job hunting, but spent most of my time keeping fit. I was a real fitness freak. I appreciated the benefits of health and fitness and the effects that exercise can have on a person's wellbeing. Although I had been running and lifting weights since I was 15, I never fully appreciated the psychological benefits exercise can have on a person until I was in my early 20's. I had just experienced the lows and frustrations of being incarcerated for months at a time. Running not only released the endorphins that gave me that feel good factor, but it gave me the ultimate appreciation of being free. I would often go running at 2:00am when no one else was around and the streets were quiet and the air was fresh. I reached a good level of fitness and was running eight to 10 miles most days. I was keen on weight training too which I'd been doing in prison and put quite a bit of muscle on. I took up karate and kung fu and I seemed to have started leading a fairly stable life. I wasn't hammering the booze as before and I was enjoying my new, athletic, and healthy lifestyle.

I made the most of my spare time while I was unemployed but giro pay day was the highlight of every fortnight for everyone. The post office queues spilled out on to the pavement as everyone crammed in to cash their benefits. Guaranteed, the pubs would be busy that day too and a good old session on the beer would follow. I amazed myself at one stage by giving up alcohol for six weeks. This was a miracle for me, but it also showed there was some sort of change coming over me and that I did possess strength of character after all. I kept my mind stimulated by going to Redcar College to study for an O Level in psychology which I really enjoyed doing. Since passing a basic English Language exam in Durham prison, I felt I was able to take my education further and I'd always had an interest in psychology too.

I also enrolled on a fitness instructor course, and one day the class spent the afternoon at Redcar Leisure Centre playing badminton while I went in the weights room. I'd over trained that day which I often did. It was a very hot day and I recall running around the college field in the afternoon, training on the weights, and then again that afternoon at the Leisure Centre. Exercise can become addictive due to the endorphins. One of the female students had taken a shine to me which was a great boost to my confidence. I hadn't been out of prison long and I was feeling a bit self-conscious. She watched me train until it was time to go back to the college. After college, I headed into Redcar High Street when I saw the same girl. She was sat on a wooden seat just outside the Clarendon Hotel with a skinhead who I noticed had tattoos around his throat and his arm around her. As I passed, I nodded to them. The skinhead gave me a sort of smirk, but thinking nothing of it, I carried on walking and joined the bus queue for Grangetown. I felt a tap on my right shoulder; it was the skinhead. He warned me of what would happen to me if I didn't leave his girlfriend alone. She wasn't his girlfriend, he was just being a pest. Having just spent over a year locked up with hundreds of idiots just like him, I lost patience and threw a punch, which he managed to duck away from. We both moved away from the bus queue and squared up just outside a shoe shop near the Clarendon Hotel. The skinny yob attempted a karate kick but I managed to grab him and hurl him to the ground. I then kneeled across him and squeezed his throat. As all typical cowards do, he raised his hands in defence and begged me not to hit him. The bully is always a coward. I allowed him to get up walk away and as he did he made an offhand comment to me in an attempt to salvage some credibility after I had just humiliated him. I went back to the bus stop and re-joined the queue, as he leaned against the other end of the bus shelter. I noticed him glance around to see where I was at one point. The girl, who had been at the centre of it all was picked up in a car by her father. Fed up of waiting for the bus, I sat on a nearby seat when another skinhead appeared in front of me. He looked down at me and tried to intimidate me saying, "Did you say you something about Redcar skins?"

 I wouldn't answer at first because I was gearing myself up for another fight, I remember thinking of punching him in the throat. Something inside of me must have settled down as I said "no", while thinking that he and his skinhead mates were pathetic. I would have smacked that idiot too had he not disappeared. I always found gangs amusing with their need to belong to a pack which merely highlighted their insecurities as men. Although I was enjoying my athletic lifestyle and new enthusiasm for education, I desperately needed work. The incident at the bus stop didn't help me settle either. I thought about touring the country to find work. Around this time, my mother's brother, Donald, became a big part of our lives. He was having a tough time because over the course of one week in 1985, he had retired from his job at the press office which meant he had to give up the house that went with the job. Then tragically, his beloved wife of 30 years, Mary, unexpectedly died of cancer. When he came into our lives, things changed for us forever. He was one of the most intelligent men I had ever met. He had two degrees in law, and anatomy and physiology, a diploma in psychology and a postgraduate medical history diploma from London University, which he achieved when he was 66. His career spanned 50 years, during which time he had gained the Fellowship of the Royal Anthropological Institute for his research on the Veda tribe of Ceylon (now Sri Lanka). He had worked for Barnado's as a child psychologist for gifted and disturbed children. He was an accomplished writer, having contributed hundreds of articles for the *Salisbury Medical Journal*, reported for the *Salisbury Journal* newspaper and worked for the *Salisbury Western Gazette*. It was his thirst for knowledge and continual educational achievements that inspired me most of all. I was still struggling to find a job with no skills or qualifications. One day, Donald suggested I go to Salisbury with him to try to find work but also keep him company since the loss of his wife. Since leaving prison, I hadn't found any work or, admittedly, looked very hard. I had criminal convictions, no qualifications and no work history. I needed a job where I could get a quick start, where I didn't need any qualifications and where they wouldn't delve into my past. It would be the catering industry that provided this opportunity. I soon realised that the catering industry was the perfect industry to start my working life. It had a high turnover of staff but there was always a job somewhere, often including accommodation, meals and usually, with an immediate start.

It was also an industry that took a person at face value and gave people a chance and as I discovered later, recognised that experience was more important than qualifications – at least in most establishments. It was my chance to build a career for myself and leave the past behind. I had my own independence, job security and pride. My only problem was that I never stayed in a job long enough to build a stable work history. I soon got tired of the long daily grind, and start looking for somewhere else to work. It was mainly because of the volatile temperament of the catering staff. However, Salisbury is where working life began for me. The South was a huge culture change and I was looking forward to the new challenges. I shared a flat with uncle Donald and we got along quite well, despite the age gap. He was 66 and I was 23, but we were good mates and we regularly went to the pub together. We had some great times and he was as energetic as anyone my own age. He had a real zest for life. He was a well-respected member of the community and since retiring from the *Salisbury Journal*, they had decided to keep him on working part time, writing his regular history column, *Curious Salisbury*, and covering the weekly court reports. In those days, the editorial staff would meet at the pub for a liquid lunch each day. The pub was an extension of the newsroom and a culture which has since long gone. He was always active and couldn't stop working. I met his circle of friends which included; local solicitors, councillors, police officers and even a high court judge once. During my time in Salisbury I met the *Only Fools and Horses* sitcom cast who had come to stay for a week to visit patients at the local spinal unit. I spoke to David Jason and Nicholas Lyndhurst in the White Hart Hotel, where they were staying. The hotel bar was usually very quiet, but during the week they were staying there, it was packed every night.

Salisbury was a quaint little town and was a huge change from back home. Unemployment was a lot lower and the dole queues were barely visible. I could see that everyone had a job and it was refreshing to find that there were jobs available; a complete contrast to Middlesbrough. Although I enjoyed the prospects the south offered, it made me sad to think that back home in the North East people didn't have the same opportunities. Salisbury had opportunities that I was looking forward to exploring. There was a buzz about the place and every morning, the town was busy with people going to work and going about their business. On Teesside, there were some days when I wouldn't see a single soul all day. Some even moved away from Teesside to seek work elsewhere as it seemed the only way.

I was still hanging around without a real purpose in life, then one day, Donald suggested I visit some hotels to enquire about job vacancies. It sounded easier than I expected, but I decided to give it a go. I went out one night for a few drinks when I came across the County Hotel. I made an enquiry at the bar and was taken to see the duty manager who offered me a job on the spot working as a kitchen porter. This was basically washing up, keeping the kitchen clean and general dogs bodying. I had discovered a niche where I could find work without the worry of my past spoiling it. In many ways, the catering industry suited me as it allowed me to travel around the UK and Europe experiencing different places. Although I hated the temperamental behaviours that came with the catering industry, I had some great times. Hotels had their own unique culture as did all the institutions including the army, prison, and hospitals. It didn't matter which hotel I worked in, I encountered the same characters in each one. This was like prison where each institution held the same kinds of people. It also reminded me of the army where I remember how soldiers spoke and behaved the same as one another.

While living in the south, there were a few things I missed from the north. It was strange how I missed the things that I'd normally taken for granted. While having my lunch at the White Horse Hotel bar where my uncle and his workmates from the *Journal* hung out every afternoon, I ordered an apple pie and custard. To the surprise of the barperson of my request she informed me that they didn't serve custard, just cream. Fish and Chip shops didn't sell mushy peas, and the pubs didn't serve lager with a frothy head.

I was still running a lot and using weights but even the gymnasiums were more up market. I couldn't find a weight training room like the ones I was used to at home with clanking barbells and dumbbells. At work, the long shifts, split shifts and weekend work were not for me. I loved the bond I had with my fellow workmates. It was like being part of a big family. We spent more time working with one another than with our own relatives. The hotel life provided me with an extended family which is what I loved about the catering industry. This came from a need to belong to a close knit group of people. Despite the long hours, I thrived on routine at first, and for that aspect, the job was perfect. The catering industry brought out all the positives and negatives of my life. I had a sense of belonging and had close friends, I was part of a social group and a uniformed brigade of chefs, but it wasn't right for me and my drinking became worse. I thought I had found my niche in life. I had a regular wage, a great social life, and some of the girls I worked with were interested in me. But I felt as though I was missing something.

I remember one day, picking up a newspaper and being shocked at the headlines about a child abuse scandal in Cleveland. I was horrified to read that such a thing was happening in my hometown, but even more horrified that innocent people were being accused of child abuse. As I opened the centre pages, I recognised someone I used to go to school with. His family was the first to get caught up in all the fiasco. The whole nightmare was compared to the Salem Witch Trials by Middlesbrough's MP, Stuart Bell. There were 121 cases of children taken from their parents. Tensions were so high, that one lady had an abortion so as not to have her child stolen from her and the stress of being wrongly accused gave one father a heart attack. There was an arson attack on one home, windows smashed, one family evacuated, while fathers, grandfathers and neighbours were falsely accused. Tension almost created riots, children were taken away without notice, sometimes in the middle of the night from families, schools and communities. There were conflicts between Cleveland Police, Cleveland Social Services and the North Regional Health Authority. There was an outcry, national debate, statements on the floor of the House of Commons and a judicial enquiry, which would be the longest in British history.

In retrospect of the Cleveland crisis, one would hope that all the failings of society and professional bodies would have brought major changes in attitudes over child abuse allegations, yet it has been repeatedly demonstrated how easy it is for someone to be falsely accused and condemned for life, while the accusers walk free and unscathed. Child abuse allegations are the witch trials of modern society with false allegations used as an excuse for vendettas in the form of vigilantism.

During my time in Salisbury, I'd had several bad mood swings and bouts of depression that became more regular, but there were deeper problems behind my inability to focus and settle. Serious personality changes were starting to come to the fore. I had already committed offences and done time, but something deeper, and more sinister was beginning to happen to me. I became more frequently depressed for little reason. I can remember feeling unbearably dysfunctional at times. It was as though a dark cloud was passing over me. Something biological was changing inside me which would make me incapable of leading a normal life at times. The level of despair I was starting to feel was extremely debilitating at times. Donald had a few contacts in the medical profession, and arranged for me to see one the country's top psychiatrists who, at first diagnosed me as a paranoid schizophrenic, but later decided I was deeply and emotionally disturbed. I had occasional angry outbursts and I knew that something wasn't right but no one could help me or tell me what was happening to me. This is where alcohol now became a sedative, rather than a social pastime. I had been drinking too much anyway, but I was still a fitness fanatic.

When I was working in Salisbury, Donald had persuaded me to be committed to The Old Manor Psychiatric Hospital for assessment. I'd been there less than an hour when a paranoid patient threatened me. I left after a heated debate with the doctor who tried to keep me in. It was a place of nightmares. I didn't like the staff either but unfortunately for me, it was a missed opportunity on being given an essential diagnosis.

13. Going 'Round the Bend'

I managed to get jobs washing up in hotels but never settled for long. I felt as though I was missing out on life when stuck in a kitchen day and night. I didn't stay in one job for more than just a few weeks, the longest was for three months. I felt I would be better suited to a nine to five job where my evenings and weekends were my own. I went back to York in 1988 in search of employment. This was the first time I'd been back since my arrest in 1983. I worked at the Dean Court Hotel for a short while as a pot washer which was a lot of fun. The staff were good people and we all socialised outside of work together.

I later started working as a doorman, firstly at the Old Orleans, which was a trendy sort of wine bar (now Tesco). Myself and an Australian lad were the first to work on the doors there. I then got work at the Railway King in George Hudson Street (now Pop World). Some of the old haunts I remember from the early 80's have since closed down or become something else such as the Pageant, just around the corner from the Railway King which is at the time of writing now the Salvation night club. The Pageant was a real spit and sawdust place, but very entertaining. Every night, the female staff would dance on top of the bar while the rest lined up behind it banging tambourines to the sound of 60's hit, *The Legend of Xanadu* by Dave Dee, Dozy, Beaky, Mick and Tich. It had a gritty, but fun atmosphere to it. Race days were the worst where mobs of gangs would descend on the City where it was guaranteed there'd be trouble somewhere. We didn't get much trouble in the Railway King, but there was usually a bit of verbal abuse when we had to turn away large groups because one or two people were wearing training shoes or jeans, but that was the dress code. It could get a bit risky as there was only two of us working on the door. Sometimes, we would have to face up to 20 drunk, boisterous men from out of town, long before CCTV. I'd had trouble outside the Railway King back in '83, when I was followed by a huge deaf man. I was 20 at the time, and as I was heading towards the bar, he latched on to me and wouldn't leave me alone. I kept indicating to him that I was heading for the bar and that he should go in a different direction. He was at least six feet tall and of large build. I knew I could be in real trouble if I didn't do something fast, so I lashed out with a punch to his rib cage and another to the jaw. He hit the ground and slumped against the railings outside the doorway. I got away fast and headed to another pub. Sometimes there is no time to dither and risk getting a beating. Hit first, has always been my motto.

Another notorious watering hole in York was Casanova's Nightclub, where I also worked as a doorman. I later learned that it was eventually closed down by the licence courts. It was at Casanovas where I also learned how to be ruthless with troublemakers because when trouble started, nobody cared who got hurt. One night, a big fight kicked off and I ended up in the middle getting punched from all angles. At this point a fellow doorman called Neil who weighed 21 stone, bear hugged the ring leader. While grappling, they both fell on to a brass tube barrier which buckled under the weight. I managed to get the culprit's arm locked and shoved up his back and hurled him out of the front door. Neil later told me that we couldn't afford to hesitate, "You have to stick your fingers in their eyes, grab hair or whatever it takes," he said. I never entered a situation on my own again after that. I can usually sense trouble brewing long before it starts, and there are so many incidents I see today where violence could be nipped in the bud. I was training on the weights a lot and gaining some real size at this time which helped a lot for the job. I used to train at Physical Wrecks Gym in Monkgate which was owned by my friend, Fred. Fred had a lot of experience of training people and helped me a lot with training and advice. The gym was host to several characters. One of the regulars was a well-known, local lad called Tony (Tote)

Claridge. He had tremendous strength and although he had a reputation for being a hard man, was actually a real gentleman; very polite and courteous. Another, was Paul Garner who had the most amazing physique winning several major body building competitions. Fred and I became very good friends and not long after, a chef who knew Fred, found me a job working as a kitchen porter at the Crest Hotel (now the Hilton), where he worked. Soon after starting there, I began dating a waitress called Denise, but it was complicated from the start. Although I was now 25, I had never had a serious girlfriend. My life had been too haywire, so I was still very emotionally inexperienced. I had slept with a prostitute when I was in the army, but that was purely for the sexual experience. I believe my inexperience was behind a lot of my relationship problems over the years; because I was a late starter. I experienced emotions I had never felt before. Denise and I first properly connected one day when I was in York Magistrates' Court, awaiting my fate for defaulting on paying a fine for a criminal damage charge. I was sat waiting in the corridor when she walked in. I noticed how sexy she looked; I was used to seeing her at work in a drab waitress uniform. Today, she wore a black two piece outfit, high heels and looked a million dollars. She'd had some things stolen by her ex-boyfriend and was there to see if they'd been recovered. She sat next to me chatting and was curious about why I was there. I explained that one night, I'd put a window through at the Tam O' Shanter pub just for the hell of it. I told her about how I was walking past the pub one night, when I got an urge to elbow one of their windows through. This was another of my most stupid ideas. I recalled how the landlord, and the regulars, came running out of the pub and gave me a good kicking and how I started attacking them back once I recovered myself. Of course, when the police arrived, all they saw was me lashing out. I was arrested that night at the scene of the crime and charged with criminal damage. I had deserved what I got though. The landlord gave some cock and bull story that the pub window was of a special make, so were more expensive than most. I was fined £300 but didn't keep up the payments, so I was hauled in front of the magistrates and ordered to continue paying instalments.

Denise was going through a trial separation with her husband. At the Crest Hotel's Christmas party, which was held in January at the Abbey Park Hotel, which is (now Ramada Jarvis Hotel), we got together. We danced, then spent the night together. Our relationship was very sexual as all my relationships were, but that night changed everything for me. The one thing that had been missing in my life was the love of a good woman. Deluded though I was, I always imagined a perfect life of going home to a loving wife and children at the end of the day. I had an idealistic image of the perfect home life I wanted, but it was never to be. Since my parents' divorce, rejection had been a difficult pill to swallow, and once I started dating girls, splitting up became something I struggled to deal with. Although I knew it was part of life, I used to take it very hard. I had been rejected by my father, my teachers, peers, girls; had no emotional strength whatsoever and couldn't handle rejection.

Looking back, all my relationships were based on sex, as much and as often as possible. I even remember a friend having a quiet word with me because Denise had confided in his wife that I was too demanding. Apparently, three times a day was too excessive. I think I was just making up for lost time, or was highly sexed myself, then again, Denise was also highly sexed. We would go anywhere and everywhere to have sex. I was always one for experimenting. We made love in horse stables where she worked, in the woods, in a shop doorway, in the back of her car. Had I just been satisfied with all this, I'm sure it would have carried on like that for years. But I was always looking for something deeper and more meaningful, or someone to make me happy. I couldn't understand why I couldn't lead a steady life like those happy couples around me. I remember feeling desperately lonely, like there was a massive hole in my life, so much so, that I could feel it in the pit of my stomach. I had massive insecurities and feelings of emptiness and I had been this way as long as I could remember. I never had a steady girlfriend, just girls who didn't want to commit, had been in bad relationships, and some, just wanted the excitement of an affair. The women I attracted were fascinated by my chequered past and spontaneity because they had led dull lives and found being with me exciting. They had no desire to settle down with me. They tended to have emotional baggage, problems, and personal issues. I was like a magnet for women like this because we connected through our shared dysfunctional lives and had so much in common. It was always a recipe for disaster.

At first, the romance was always exciting and passionate and we couldn't get enough of one another, but as fast as my so called relationships began, they fizzled out. I couldn't handle flirtatiousness either. Denise was a flirt which caused a lot of arguments. I yearned for stability and family life that was taken from me as a boy. My mood swings were unpredictable and rejection from a girl I liked would be enough to send me into a deep, alcohol fuelled depression. The only self-esteem I had was through working out in the gym to build the perfect physique. I was a gym freak and over the years had trained hard to get a muscular frame. On the outside, I was seen as a powerful man who had endured all sorts of hardships in life and someone who could take care of women and protect them. Women always assumed that because I looked tough outwardly, inside I would be the same. This could not have been further from the truth and that was the problem. Inside I was an emotional wreck, incapable of having a real relationship. Once a woman saw how unstable and clingy I was, they lost interest, then I would try to fix it and be the strong man they wanted, but I wasn't really that man. I was weak, and vulnerable, and they didn't want another child, as many told me over the years, they wanted a man. This just made me feel even more inadequate.

I was a desperately unhappy person and my depressions started to get worse. One Saturday, I remember being at home and feeling intensely sad and lonely. I had been looking forward to Denise coming to see me, but she didn't contact me when she said she would. The feeling of abandonment was so strong, I took a razor and cut deep into my wrists slashing them ten times. When I woke the next morning, I was surrounded by blood on the floor and all over my sheets. I managed to get myself ready and go to work at Physical Wrecks where I'd been covering some shifts for Fred. I felt drowsy and drained. I phoned Fred, and asked him to come and see me. As I unwrapped my bandaged wrists to show him what I'd done, he almost threw up. The insides of my wrists were exposed where I'd hacked away. He took me straight to York District Hospital, where I spent several days being stitched up and assessed by a psychiatrist. I never told Denise why I had slashed my wrists; I was too embarrassed.

As my relationship with Denise developed, she left her husband and divorced him. We moved in together in a double room of a shared house in Scarcroft Road. It was too much of an upheaval for Denise. I knew she was getting itchy feet by the way she was talking and I started to become possessive and paranoid that she was going to leave me. She was unable to live with the fact that her kids were with her ex-husband. I was too immature to understand how much this must have affected her at the time. Denise missed her kids and I was suffocating her. One day, after an argument, I threw a hot frying pan against the kitchen wall. At that point, Denise had taken as much as she could and walked out on me. Two days later, I came home after spending all day drinking myself into oblivion. I went to our bedroom and the first thing I saw was the empty wardrobe. She'd gone back to the house, packed most of her stuff and left while I was out. I started to turn things over in my mind, I started to think about some of her friends who worked at the Crest Hotel, perhaps they had influenced her decision to leave me. I knew she kept in touch with her former colleagues and I knew that some of them disapproved of our relationship. I felt that quite a few of her friends had it in for me. My paranoia was out of control now. The landlord who we were renting the room from kept a high powered air rifle which he normally kept locked away. That night I saw it leaning against the living room wall wrapped in a cloth cover. I grabbed it and headed off to the hotel in search of some kind of revenge. I didn't know what I was going to do, I didn't have a plan. My mind was racing. I was hurting and drunk. Walking through the streets late at night carrying a loaded rifle without a care in the world, I stormed into the Crest Hotel foyer where Fred was now working as a night porter since selling his gym. He tried talking me into handing over the rifle, at which point, I pointed it at him. It was loaded and the safety catch was off. The result could have been devastating.

It was only recently I learned of this from Fred after I tracked him down 23 years later. My mind had blocked this episode out for over 20 years but why on earth would I do this to a good friend? I still have no recollection of doing it. Fred told me that I was completely out of it by then and had no idea what I was doing. Ironically, only minutes after that episode, a swarm of police officers entered the foyer but only for a party. Talk about getting away by the skin of my teeth!

That night Fred drove me to Bootham Park Psychiatric Hospital. He hammered on the main door of the hospital demanding someone help me. A male nurse came to the door who just kept telling him that I needed to make an appointment with my GP first. Fred decided to take the nurse to his car, where he opened the boot and showed him the rifle. It must have had the desired effect because I was admitted and led to one of the wards. In that state of mind, I don't understand how I could be expected to hold on for several days for a GP's appointment and then go on a waiting list for an appointment to see a specialist. They had just wanted to send me home. Several months before, I had slashed my wrists 10 times and now I had just walked into a hotel lobby with a rifle. What more evidence did they need that I was in a very disturbed state of mind? This is one of the most ludicrous policies of the medical health system that when someone is in their most desperate mental state, they are expected to calmly make a doctor's appointment and wait!

Bootham was an old Victorian asylum with huge corridors and very similar to St Luke's. The driveway within the hospital grounds, bended and curved around leading to the doorway. Bends were always placed in the entrance drives of Victorian mental hospitals to differentiate them from the stately homes of the gentry, which usually had straight drives, hence the term, 'going round the bend'.

I was in there for about four days spending most of my time thinking about Denise. I sneaked out of the hospital grounds one evening and got a taxi to Denise's house several miles away. She had gone to back to her marital home, although not as a wife. When I turned up on her doorstep, it was as though they had been expecting me. Her ex-husband was quite courteous and invited me in. Denise came through and held my hands. "Look at his eyes," she said, "They're all puffed up!" I felt some relief after seeing her and was pleased there was no aggro. I got a taxi back to the hospital and as I walked back on to the ward, the charge nurse saw me from her office and sarcastically asked, "Did you enjoy your trip, David?" I can't remember if I answered.

I didn't think much of the ward staff to be honest - they were hopeless with patients. We were ignored and left to sit around all day tormented and desperate for help. We were like domestic animals being farmed. We all seemed to be waiting for something, but never knew what. I was starting to realise that being an inpatient did more harm than good to a person's soul. The next day, I found a phone book in the hospital's public phone booth. I thumbed through the pages until I had found what I hoped was Denise's home phone number and rang her. I had got the right number. I could tell in her voice that she was really happy to hear from me which helped me recover quickly as my depression lifted. Soon after, she came to visit me which lifted my spirits more. I was discharged from hospital not long after and soon we were living together again. It wasn't to last though and after a few weeks, she left me again. One day, I blew my top during a row and punched the bedroom door leaving it hanging from its hinges. Denise walked out again. This became a pattern for Denise. Whenever we had a row, she would walk out, come back and then after several weeks, disappear again. Every time she came back to me, I became more possessive and paranoid because I was always on tenterhooks expecting her to leave again. Repeating what I did the last time she left me, I went out on a drinking binge session one afternoon, but this time in the middle of her carrying her clothes and belongings to a removal van with her ex-husband in tow. I noticed there was a police car outside she had called knowing I would kick off. I went to warn the officer to stay out of our business which only fuelled the situation. I was emotionally wrecked. I ran upstairs and started smashing things up in the bedroom. The police officer appeared and managed to get me in a tight headlock that felt as though it was going to pull my head off. Shortly afterwards, two detectives arrived on the scene, bundled me into the back of a van and drove me to York Police Station.

Fred came to my rescue again and asked the police if they would let me go on condition he drove me back to Middlesbrough. They agreed and Fred had me home in just over an hour. I felt a sense of relief being home again, even though I was hurting inside a lot. I had no coping mechanisms. One thing I did have to cling on to though, was a burning ambition to be a successful chef and it was ambition that got me through the hardest periods of my life.

At work, I was able to focus my mind on something positive because when I was in York, I'd started training to be a chef. One good thing that had come from my relationship with Denise was that she had persuaded me to take a job as a Breakfast Chef at the Abbey Park Hotel which started my transition from pot washer to trainee Chef. I then worked at the Royal York Hotel and from then on, my culinary career took off. Unfortunately, chefs were noted in those days for being heavy drinkers and it seemed that I would follow suit.

14. The 'Demon Drink'

Whenever I had problems, I would always turn to alcohol. Eventually, I became dependent on it. I couldn't face anything without it. I would always use it as an escape from reality, and sometimes as an excuse to cause trouble fuelled with Dutch courage. I would then blame others for making me do it - a classic trait among many persistent offenders. Once I started going straight and had turned my life around, I started to self reflect a lot more, particularly focussing on aspects of my behaviour, lifestyle and the role alcohol played in it. There were many positives to my association with alcohol and pub life, but there were also many negatives. Sometimes, I would drink so much I would get into a fight, be asked to leave, or be thrown out of a pub. But pubs also provided me with an income where I would often do the cooking, but I just couldn't get the balance right. I always preferred to drink within social settings. I never drank in the house as this defeated the object for me and I never drank spirits. I belonged to the culture labelled in the 1990's as lager louts. Because of the nature of my work, I was able to move from town to town taking up new jobs and wherever I was I'd loved to pub crawl and visit the inns and taverns around me.

When I found work in Edinburgh in 1992, I was on the verge of a serious drink problem coinciding with regular bouts of depression. Yet I still somehow managed to keep getting employment albeit never for very long. I worked at a quaint, 15th century pub called Ye Olde Golf Tavern.

Edinburgh was a fascinating place, steeped in history as well as having a vibrant modern life with all the excitement I needed. It was also over run with football hooligan casuals from Hibs and Hearts. Not being a football fan, I was uninterested in this, but I remember them in the pubs I used. I never had any trouble with any of them myself and it was only later that I learned how huge this following was. Edinburgh was also where I was introduced to late drinking hours which would be one of the worst things that could have happened to me. I enjoyed working at the Tavern, but it was clear that alcohol was becoming a major problem in my life. I had regular money coming in but every penny went on booze.

I had never been to bars that stayed open until 2:00am, or nightclubs that stayed open until 6:00am. Some of the pubs opened at 6:00am too. This was a real novelty. It was while I was working here that the Scottish licensing laws extended day time drinking hours from 11:00am to 11:00pm. Therefore, effectively, in Edinburgh, it was possible to drink around the clock in the town centre. As with my uncle's journalist drinking culture, the catering industry had the very same reputation, particularly amongst chefs. Even the chef I worked with supped cans of beer while working the breakfast shift beginning from 6:00am.

Things got so bad that once, when I was working the breakfast shift, I went straight to work from a nightclub. I had been drinking all night and was still under the influence when I turned up for work. I hadn't even been to bed. The manager wasn't impressed at all.

Some nights, I only grabbed a few hours' sleep and hadn't showered from the night before. I used to leave work, hot and sticky from the kitchen and in need of a shower but instead, I would go clubbing until the early hours. By the time I got home, I would be so exhausted from the 12 hour shift I'd worked, followed by a binge that I would fall asleep straight away. The next morning, I would have to drag myself out of bed early to unlock the Tavern so the cleaners could get in, while suffering a hangover.

I felt that working in Scotland was perfect for me because of the extended pub opening hours. I loved the Scottish way of life. The Scots seemed more laid back than the English. They got their work done and still always had time to party. They had a lovely, warm attitude to life. One New Year's Eve (Hogmanay), I had the best time ever. I had heard that the Scottish made a big thing about New Year and had seen it on television at home, but this was something else. I had never seen a New Year celebration like it.

But no sooner had I begun to settle into one job, I would be looking for another. I worked daily split shifts between 10.00am and 2.00pm then go back at 6.00pm until around 10.00pm. Rather than go back to an empty flat for those four hours in between shifts, I used to go to the pub. I often went back to work worse for wear, trying to perform my duties in the kitchen, reeking of beer. At the end of the shift, I would help to clean up and go for a late drink at a bar, or nightclub. I repeated this process every night.

Pubs were full of characters, excitement and unpredictability, but alcohol controlled me. I drank every day, and as often as possible. After working in too many jobs to remember during the 1990's and blowing all my money through my alcohol addiction, I went back to Middlesbrough for a while. One day, I received a call from a company called PGL, who run children's groups, providing activity courses and holidays. I had applied for seasonal work as a chef when they rang me to offer me a job in Northern France. Of course, I jumped at the chance. In those days, 12 month passports could be bought from the Post Office, so as soon as I could get one, I did. France was very laid back, and great fun. I was living in an old hotel called Le Pre Catalane in Hardelot which PGL had converted into dormitories for school tours.

The people I worked with were students, either on placements, or taking a year out of study to work with the kids. They used to teach them things like archery, horse riding, go-karting, and take them on days out. One day when they went on a day trip to Paris, I tagged along. It was fantastic. I became quite proficient at speaking French because I mixed a lot with the locals whereas my English work colleagues just tended to mix with each other. I felt that in order to enjoy another culture and learn about it, I should integrate with the locals. Then I made the same old mistake. I met a local girl called Sandrine who was a young, sexy, 23 year old French girl who worked at a local restaurant where I used to go drinking. She was married, as Denise had been, but also going through a separation. We hit it off straight away after she followed me one day and invited me to go for a drink. It was passionate from the start. We would make love all day long, or if the coast was clear, we would spend nights of passion at her flat in Boulogne. The season was coming to a close and I was offered a chance to stay on through the winter months as caretaker, so we would soon have more time to spend together, or so I'd thought. I was in the same trap as I had been with Denise. Things didn't work out with Sandrine. She patched things up with her husband. She came to see me one day to end it and I never saw her again.

Hardelot was a seasonal town which practically closed down in winter time and I was bored to tears. This was also a pattern that had developed within me over the years - an inability to deal with boredom. The loneliness and sadness affected me badly and I had one of my worst depressive episodes. Whenever I'd had episodes before, I had friends and family around me, now I was all alone in a huge Victorian hotel in the north of France. There wasn't soul in sight. It had all the ambience for a remake of *The Shining* and I was heading for another breakdown. There were hundreds of cases of wine in the kitchen which I set about drinking by the gallon. The winter weather with its howling winds had now began which was a complete contrast to the summer months. Only weeks before the weather was bright and the hotel lively with staff and kids everywhere. Everything banged or rattled with the wind and I was feeling unbelievably isolated. I had no company and I was spooked by the place. I kept thinking of the hotel's history. It was once occupied by the German army during the First World War and one of the previous owners had been killed there after falling down the stairs.

At one point I rang the French Foreign Legion recruitment office in Lille. The poster on the office wall, where I got the number from, said that they accepted recruits up to 40 years old, so I rang them and asked to join. I was told to call back and speak to Le Capitan on Monday morning. I didn't ring again.

Another day, I chased an army *Land Rover* which had several military personnel sitting in the back. They realised I was trying to speak to them and the vehicle slowed down. I asked them to take me with them when I finally caught up with them but they weren't Legionnaires. My mind was playing tricks on me and a deep paranoia had now set in. Over the years I had always had problems with depression but at some stage in my life, I also developed paranoia. I jumped at every single sound and after weeks of drunkenness and pining for Sandrine, I cut myself up again. Self-harming was the way I dealt with pain. I smashed the kitchen window and cut myself with a piece of glass I picked up from the floor. There was glass and blood everywhere.

I decided to admit myself to the psychiatric hospital in Boulogne, which was difficult because of the language barrier. It was Christmas time and I wanted to be at home with people I knew. I remember feeling as though as I was in a deep, black hole with no way out. This was one of my darkest moments of depression. This time, my medication was a tranquilliser in the form of a syringe. I wandered off the ward one day and went to the canteen until someone called to have me taken back to the ward. I remember begging the nurse to inject me because I was feeling desperately sad. Three days later, I was taken back to the hotel, but I knew I had to get back to England.

Mixing with locals during the summer had paid off for me because when I needed help, one of them gave me the money for a ferry back to England. Once I was home, I was seen by my doctor, who referred me to St Luke's Psychiatric Hospital on New Year's Eve 1992. After five days, I was released with more anti-depressants. Being home helped me start my recovery slowly, then several months later, I found work again out of the area.

Over the years I worked as chef, I saw lots of wonderful places such as York, Edinburgh, France, Corsica, Isle of Wight, the Lake District, and the Scottish Highlands. I made hundreds of friends and had a girl in every port. However, I squandered every penny I earned. I partied every night and burned the candle at both ends. Wherever I worked during the summer months, I treated it as a holiday and as though every day was my last. I would never recover from the long term effect this had on my life. Because I never looked after money nor ever saved a single penny, I was never in a position to get a mortgage or be able to afford to rent a flat or house.

I had managed to go full circle with my life. I had started with nothing, had it and lost it. I had been given the chance to build a successful career as a chef and leave the past behind but I had blown it. Now I was back where I started. I was once again living on Teesside, with no job. I was better off than I was when I started, in the sense that I was now an experienced chef, but I had no goal or purpose in life. I continued to be a drifter.

15. Armed and Dangerous

It was during the early 1990's while living back on Teesside, I noticed a new culture emerging that would start to shape our current problems in society. In Grangetown and surrounding areas, where I had spent most of my youth, things started to change for the worse as the birth of the Anti-Social Behaviour Order (ASBO) culture emerged. It was a culture of anti-social families who were hell bent on ruining other people's lives and criminals, who were getting younger and younger. It was now 1993 and our area was no longer the peaceful, close knit community anymore, but a place of fear. Drugs were rife and an anti-social culture was emerging with little or no respect for people, or property and certainly no fear of authority. The area had been ruined in just a matter of months. Neighbours who had never needed to worry, now lived in constant fear. Law abiding citizens now had to protect themselves and their property as burglaries and thefts increased. I needed to escape the area. I knew I would get into trouble if I didn't, so I continued looking for jobs in other places.

I started carrying a loaded handgun and a knife around with me. One night I went to Bennett's night club in South Bank with the gun inside my jacket, doing little to hide it. As I left the club, I was confronted by the police Armed Response Unit who yelled at me to get on my knees with my hands against the wall. I felt something pointing in the back of my head while they removed my gun. I kept asking the officer who had grassed on me and all he said was, "Think about David."

That was enough for me, I knew who had done it. I was then taken to South Bank Police Station where I was charged with being drunk and disorderly and in possession of a loaded firearm. I was later bailed to appear in court at a later date. During my time on bail, I contacted an old friend I had worked with in France. He now lived in a nice part of Somerset, called Wells. He invited me to go and stay with him to see if I could find work, which I did almost straight away. This helped me when I had to return to Middlesbrough to appear in court. I decided that as I got to know my work colleagues more, I could confide in them about my forthcoming court appearance back home. I came clean to my employers too who were very understanding and gave me the day off to travel the long journey from the West country to the North East to attend court. They even provided me with character references. I believe it was because of this, I received a heavy fine, rather than imprisonment. Having a regular job and good character references to present to the court was usually the difference between being handed a prison sentence or a fine. I returned to Wells a very relieved person.

One day, my mother telephoned to tell me she had been burgled by a low life who had kicked her front door in while she and Donald were visiting York for the day. Donald had some of his wife's irreplaceable jewellery stolen too and I was worried for their safety. Youths had been throwing stones at their windows, wrecking the fence and starting small fires. They had no morals or decency, terrorising two elderly people. It wasn't just my mother's house they targeted. Others became victims of these low lives. I rang the police on numerous occasions, but they did absolutely nothing. Myself and others in the area had called the police so many times yet no action was taken. One day I spoke to the police officer who covered our area about my concerns who said to me, "Well they have windows too." This was a first. I had practically been given permission to commit a criminal act by a police officer. This made me despise certain criminal types that prey on the innocent and vulnerable.

I tried to set up a protection racket and vigilante group. The drug culture was emerging fast and I wanted to start protecting the innocent. Too many good people were having their lives ruined by immoral arseholes. Nobody was interested in helping me. My associates were all settled, married men now. I approached the hardest and the most ruthless, but it seemed that the old school were fist fighters, not shooters. I had always used knives in the past, now I was into guns. I didn't care about the pain I inflicted on others. I was venting my own pain and suffering at the world, but only on those I felt deserved it.

16. Paranoia and Persecution

It was clear that this new yob culture was something that the police hadn't been prepared for, so the law didn't protect the innocent. Thankfully, my mother was able to convince the local council that they needed to move her and uncle Donald to a nicer area. They gave her a bungalow in Lingdale, East Cleveland. It was a lot smaller, but safer and the area seemed quiet. The scenery was beautiful and I could see why some people would want to live in the countryside. I was aggressive looking and quite unapproachable, so I didn't fit in. I was of massive build, constantly frowned and displayed general hostility so my whole demeanour was quite intimidating. That is how the locals described me when I was arrested several months down the line.

I had just come from an area where my mother and uncle, now in their 70's, were driven from their home by yobs and failed by an invisible police presence. I was suspicious of everyone, angry that I was unable to protect my mother and constantly on guard. I brought all this with me to East Cleveland. I didn't attempt to fit in which is a shame, because had I given the place a chance, things may not have turned out as they did. I was a different person then, even my own mother said I had evil eyes. But while I was hostile to others, they were also hostile towards me and no one tried to befriend me, or get to know the real David. I had come from Grangetown, so I was called a 'townie' and shunned by the locals, making me feel paranoid and bitter.

At least, that's how it all felt at the time. The Lingdale Tavern was our local pub. It had a reputation for great food with people visiting from all over. It reminded me of the old taverns in horror movies, when the whole place falls silent as a stranger enters and is greeted

with icy stares. The nearest village to Lingdale was Boosbeck. This place was even worse. There were two pubs known as the bottom house, (Station Hotel) and the top house (The Boosbeck Hotel). This was where I got a real taste of village mentality with small minded people
making generalisations of a stranger. Although I am sure that this was not the case for everyone, this is how I remember it. Those who showed animosity towards me, used to all congregate in The Station every karaoke night. There was a clear disregard for outsiders from some of the locals. It was extremely cliquey. There were one or two pubs which encouraged this and attracted the most bigoted. Regulars were served before those who weren't part of the clique which used to really annoy me, but not as much as the way Donald was treated.
 Donald was one of the most educated people they were ever likely to meet in their lives, but they ridiculed him behind his back. They didn't believe, or more likely were unable to comprehend that someone had done so many things and achieved so much in one lifetime. They had probably never travelled outside their village. Had they been able to listen and take in all of his stories, they may have learned something from a man who had travelled the world, spoke seven languages and worked hard for his many degrees. I regret that Donald was brought to this place. The people weren't prepared to understand those who spoke and behaved differently and Donald quickly gave up. Without his friends from Salisbury, he was excluded, didn't fit in, and his health went rapidly downhill during his final years.

In time, I started to settle and enrolled at Prior Pursglove College in Guisborough, to study A Level psychology, and GCSE French. I was able to mix with a different group of people. I didn't finish the course as access courses had become popular. They were for people who wanted to go to university but didn't have A Levels. I enrolled at Redcar College, but when I failed the exam, I became depressed and started drinking more. I found work on the Scottish borders as a chef at a pub called The Dolphin in Eyemouth. I was still keeping fit too at the local boxing club and swimming, where I tried to learn how to scuba dive.

Bev was a landlady at a nearby pub called The Wheel Hotel. I was 30, she was 47, but the age difference was all we had in common. I stayed at the pub with her, but I was a jealous person. After becoming angry about comments made to her by customers, she asked me not to use the bar, despite that I was living above the pub with her.

Jim Moorland owned The Wheel. He was a vicious, arrogant, alcoholic who liked to throw his weight around and bully people. He had little respect from others because whenever he hit the bottle he would embarrass himself. He offered to let me lease a café that he owned. I ran it for a few days with some staff members of his. I got rid of a lot of outdated stock one day, and he went mad. He shouted at me to go back to The Wheel and leave. I moved out once I was ready. Soon after, Bev and I split up, and I took it quite badly. I found work in Gloucestershire for a while, I hoped I could snap out of it. Depression doesn't work like that, so, of course, it didn't work. I was living in shared digs and working in a busy restaurant, but still felt isolated and alone. After three weeks, I returned home to Lingdale to stay with my mother and Donald, and went to see my doctor, who prescribed Seroxat anti-depressants in the hope that I could get back to my old self again.

I made friends with a couple in Boosbeck called Brian and Dawn at one of the local pubs. Dawn took a shine to me and would rub her leg against me under the table even though Brian was sitting right next to her. Naturally, I was flattered by the attention but wasn't sure what to do. I felt really uncomfortable. I wondered if they had an open relationship because she was flirting with me right under his nose. One night at The Station Hotel, Dawn came to tell me they had fallen out and were no longer an item. We spent the night together but she had done this to spite him after their argument. I was a marked man now.

I had slept with a friend's girlfriend, I wasn't local, and as word travels fast in small places, everyone soon knew. I was a complete outcast now. I handled this very badly. One night, I was in the pub toilets of the Boosbeck Hotel washing my hands and when I turned around Brian was stood blocking the doorway. He had already tried to quiz me about what happened between Dawn and I earlier that night. Refusing to go into detail, I told him I didn't want to hurt his feelings. Now he was blocking the way out of the toilet so I squared up to fight him. At this point, the landlord pushed open the door and defused the situation telling Brian to go back to the bar. As I left the toilet, several others were waiting outside ready to back Brian up. I heard Brian mutter that he would get me next time. Over the next 24 hours, his comment sent me into a state of acute paranoia.

I had never had such strong feelings of hopelessness before. I felt trapped with feelings that were so bizarre. With repressed emotions and feelings of paranoia and persecution, I spent a whole day drinking around Guisborough telling everyone that I intended to sort Brian out. I went home early that evening and slept off the beer. It wasn't enough though to shake off the dark, desperate feelings of no-return.

That night, I decided to go and look for Brian at The Station Hotel where I knew he would be. I felt a deep sadness as I left the house and said goodbye to my mother and Donald. I knew I wouldn't be seeing them for quite a while as I set off on the mile and a half long walk towards Boosbeck. The Station was very busy that night. As I walked in, I saw Brian sat at the bar. We caught each other's eye. I only drank one or two pints, but I was topping up what I'd consumed earlier. I decided to approach him head on and confront him over his threats. I was already feeling very depressed about being excluded by the local community. He didn't react well to this and a violent exchange ensued.

What had possessed me to do this? Why didn't I just stay away from these places and let the dust settle? Was I provoking the situation? Or was I an innocent caught up in it all?

The police turned up at the wrong pub at first. They went to The Station Hotel in Loftus, but eventually turned up when they handcuffed me and led me from the pub. As I left with the cigarette dangling from the corner of my mouth, I turned to the landlord who was watching from behind the bar and said: "See you soon, Martin." Months later, when I was reading my forthcoming trial depositions in prison, Martin had said in his statement: "I thought it was a strange thing to do."

18 years have passed since that night and it feels as though I'm telling someone else's story. I can't comprehend my motives or the person I was. I have absolutely no connection whatsoever to that person.

The landlady had told the police that I was always staring at her but she did have a high opinion of herself. I disliked her type and would often wonder what a nice guy like Martin was doing with her. I actually felt sorry for him because he was a nice lad and didn't deserve any of this. Everyone interviewed by the police told them that I was always staring at people. I've always been a people watcher. That's why I became a social scientist. I was constantly observing individuals and their behaviours.

That night, while sat in the back of the police van, one of the officers standing outside called out to me: "Is this your usual forte, Honeywell?"

He then went back inside the pub to get witness statements. As I waited with the other officer in the back of the van with the doors wide open, I saw paramedics carrying a stretcher with Brian on to the ambulance. I was taken to South Bank Police station for heavy questioning the next day. The police don't waste their time questioning someone who has had a skin full of booze. They leave you to sleep it off in a cell before meeting your solicitor the next morning. Unlike previous arrests, all my clothes were removed and taken for forensic evidence. I was given some white disposable coveralls with slippers to match. The coveralls were very hot and I was constantly sweating. It was a hot July day and bizarrely, exactly 10 years to the day since I was released from Durham Prison. They took a saliva swab from inside my mouth and explained that if I was found not guilty, it would be destroyed.

By the tone of questioning from CID, it was inevitable that I was going to get the book thrown at me. I was charged with attempted murder. They had tried to use the fact I'd told the landlady to call the police and not an ambulance as my way of hoping he wouldn't survive the attack. I expected about 10 years in prison for this and I showed no remorse at the time. While I was sat in Guisborough cells, I could hear the officers talking to each other. I remember wishing I could have turned out like them and lived a normal life with a good career. I never had an issue with the police. They had a job to do and that's all there was to it. Meanwhile, my mother had the police at her house, searching for my antidepressants.

Feelings were running high locally, so I was flanked by several police officers in court the next day and not surprisingly, there was no application for bail. I was remanded for three weeks and taken to Holme House Prison.

17. Changing Prison Culture

HMP Holme House was a fairly new prison in 1995. It had four house blocks and housed both remand and convicted prisoners on separate blocks. The convicted block was nicknamed 'the dark side'. Two police officers took me to the reception entrance where I was processed. Inside, there were other prisoners also waiting and I noticed to my left, a small room with a few prisoners inside who didn't seem to belong. I later discovered they were sex offenders.

The handcuffs, which had cut deep into my wrists, leaving a red groove were unlocked and removed by one of the police officers. I was then ceremoniously handed over to Her Majesty's Prison Service. I noticed another much larger room which was a holding cell opposite the reception desk. It was full of other prisoners waiting to be allocated to their cells which offered more comfort than being herded around like sheep in reception.

I was taken to the holding cell which had plastic windows, had no ventilation and got quite cramped as it filled up. We were crammed in like sardines. I hadn't been there 10 minutes when I recognised some familiar faces from my time in Durham and Low Newton a decade earlier. They recognised me too, nodding and acknowledging me. It was as though I had never left. It also made me realise that should I ever upset anyone in prison, it would catch up with me as my face would always be recognised by someone. Eventually, my name was called to go back to reception where my property was emptied on the desk in front of me from a large polythene bag. Each item was recorded on a form. They then handed me the items I was allowed to keep and confiscated the rest. They took my finger prints again even though the police had already taken them. Once they were finished, was told I was allowed to still wear my own clothes because

I was on remand. Prison had changed in many ways, but in other ways, time had stood still. The staff and inmate culture had changed beyond recognition, yet some of the same procedures had remained the same. The familiar prison slang was coming back to me, it was still the same, but with a few additional modern terms. Prison slang is like its own language.

Prisoners still ranted on about how they would be out in a few weeks; how they were innocent; and how they had been framed by the police or 'grassed up' by someone. A doctor (now prisoner) was sitting directly opposite me who had been charged for selling prescriptions to drug users. I noticed he was wearing a rather expensive gold watch and I remember thinking that it wouldn't be in his possession for long once the bullies spotted it. I also noticed a few of the prisoners were holding electrical radios and tape recorders they had brought with them. I was a bit baffled because when I left prison all those years ago, we were only allowed battery operated radios.

Obviously, these lads knew the score and had made sure they had such luxuries during their stay in prison. Before being transferred to prison, families can take requested items to the police station which are then put into polythene bags and taken with the prisoner in the police van. It is then reviewed in reception to see if it can be taken into the prison, left in property for collection on release, or confiscated altogether. For example, I had an aerosol of shaving foam which was confiscated because it could be used to spray at someone. The bags were then fastened tight with a security tag. Security tags were used on everything, including electrical goods. This was to ensure that if something was stolen from your cell it could be traced. It was also to trace items that were sold, as this was against regulations and resulted in punishment.

I was experiencing similar emotions to prisoners who struggle to readjust to all the new changes in the outside world after serving a long stretch. I was trying to readjust to all the changes that had taken place on the inside world, after a long stint outside. We were allocated cell numbers and landings and our own personal identification numbers which is what we had now become - a number. I was no longer a person. I was taken to the hospital wing to be assessed as to whether I was suicidal or a danger to others due to my history of depression. The next day I was taken to see the doctor. I noticed on his desk was my box of antidepressants. After the police collected them from my mother's home, they handed them to the prison staff who then passed them on to the hospital staff. The doctor examined the box then threw them to one side, telling me that I didn't need them. Later, I learned that there had been some research into Seroxat after people had complained of serious side effects including, suicidal thoughts, aggression and increased depression. The doctor may have actually been doing me a favour.

There were some very odd characters on the hospital wing and as in 1983 during my stint in Thorpe Arch prison's hospital wing, I was oblivious to most of the others' backgrounds. I was sharing a cell with a young lad who suffered from epilepsy. They deliberately put him in with me as they felt I was sensible enough to take care of him if he had an attack, I don't know what he was in for and we didn't talk about those things on the hospital wing.

Bored and restless, I would wander around the corridors and chat to people. I later discovered that on the wing, there was a paedophile ring, a former prison officer who had chopped his wife into pieces and someone who I recognised from the television who had torched his house, killing his three kids.

One day, as I was walking along the corridor, a prisoner called out to me from the open food hatch of his cell door and asked me for a cigarette. I had noticed that he was always behind his door but hadn't given it a second thought. I handed him a cigarette at which point a male nurse approached warning me not to go anywhere near him again. I could see in his eyes that he was trying to tell me something but wasn't allowed to explain why he had made such a statement. He said: "He is a very nasty piece of work. Stay well away from him!"

I did as he said and it turned out that the prisoner was a brutal rapist who had infected one of his cellmates after raping him too. Had anyone ever tried that with me, I would have killed them without giving it a second thought. Thankfully, I wasn't on the hospital wing very long. I was interviewed with the prison psychiatrist who felt I was fit to be sent to the remand wing. I was then transferred to A2 landing, House Block Two. Once I was there, I made my mind up to continue my studies. I had a genuine fascination with human behaviour and because I had been studying psychology at college, I continued working towards an A Level through the education department. I waded through Richard Gross's book, *Psychology: The Science of Mind and Behaviour,* which I had been reading in the police cells. I had asked Uncle Donald to drop it off for me when I was allowed a phone call. "Here's some light reading for you, Honeywell," the police officer said. The book gave me some interesting insight into people's behaviour which I could see in my fellow inmates, myself, prison officers and other staff.

I was surprised to see how lax things had become over the years. Remand prisoners walked around wearing Bermuda shorts and flip-flops as though they were on holiday somewhere. I am sure many would argue that prisons are like holiday camps but only those who have never served time in a prison would say this. I think that the prisoners were just exploiting their right to wear what they were allowed to while on remand. It was a hot summer too at the back end of July 95.

One thing I learned was that unfortunately, prison is an occupational hazard to most criminals. I saw many brought to the landing after being remanded full of pride at being locked up again with their mates.

There's an old saying in prison; 'There's hard time and there's easy time.' In my experience, there's some truth in this saying.

There's also another saying, 'If you can't do the time, don't do the crime'. It amazed me how prisoners adopted their own hierarchy of who should rank where within the prison culture league. They thought that this hierarchy justified them to meter out punishments to prisoners they felt were beneath them. Yet, all crimes, no matter how large or small, have victims. I didn't think that any prisoner had a right to decide who was punished, or to set themselves above others.

On the remand wing, I saw men scalded, beaten and attacked because of their crimes - some of who went on to be acquitted at court because of their innocence. One man was continually attacked by other prisoners because he was charged with rape. He repeatedly swore his innocence and took a personal stand against his attackers by refusing to go on Rule 43 (VP) vulnerable prisoner wing.

Rule 43 (now called Prison Rule 45), was the term for protection and those on it would be housed on a segregated block. Prisoners could request to be placed on it for their own safety.

When the man accused of rape went to trial, his victim admitted she had lied, so he was acquitted. Prisoners know better than anyone what false allegations can do to a person, yet they never give their fellow inmates the benefit of the doubt. Punishment from other prisoners is far worse than what most of the general public would meter out.

There was another incident aimed at a man who was accused of hurting a baby. The inmates would shout at him through their bars at night. One day, when leaving the exercise yard, a crowd gathered to watch him being kicked and beaten. When one of the screws checked the lad's record, we found out that it wasn't true. It made me realise that attacks in prison were highly unpredictable, and often carried out without any thought. There was too much brainless behaviour in prison. One night, a young lad kept everyone awake all through the night by hammering on his cell door and screaming at the top of his voice. People shouted at him to shut up, but he just shouted back hurling insults. The next morning while we all queued for breakfast, tired and edgy, an older prisoner remembered one of the insults thrown at him and gave the lad a slap across the face. I was expecting the screws to intervene, but when I looked over at them, they just laughed and turned a blind eye. They must have known that he'd kept us all up. Sometimes it was easier for the screws to just turn a blind eye. There were times when I wondered if some of the screws were that much different from us. One evening, during association time, there was shouting and banging coming from inside the pool room of the opposite house block. That section of the landing was separated from ours with steel barred gates. I saw a prisoner come flying out of the pool room door and fall to his knees after being struck with a pool cue. Someone then threw a pint mug of scalding water into another man's face. I heard that this had happened because the scalded prisoner was accused of kidnapping his own children and when the police caught up with him, he'd left them locked in the boot of his car while he made a run for it.

The screws from our landing were like lightening as they bolted across to deal with the furore. The most alarming thing was that there wasn't a single screw in sight where the trouble had taken place. The screw who was overseeing the other house block, had deliberately wandered off somewhere knowing what was about to happen. A lot of people would be surprised that a prison officer would do such a thing. When I was in court waiting to be sentenced, one of the screws asked me if I would attack one of the other prisoners for him because he had swindled his mother in law out of some money. I didn't of course. I had more sense.

Most prisoners just want to get their heads down and do their time. Prisoners with the longest sentences just seem to get on with it. Most screws do their jobs well, they're easy to talk to and very helpful. Like any job though, there were a few bad apples. I felt that the Probation Service were naïve too. Once, I took part in a group discussion about offending behaviour. The group leader, a probation officer, told us that there were alternatives to offending, that we had a choice. I challenged this because there are many situations where a person may have to offend to protect themselves or their property. For example, if someone entered my home, I would feel justified in doing what was necessary to protect myself and my family. What would be the alternative in that situation? Wait to see what they do to you and your family?

I came across a couple of screws in Holme House who were old friends of mine from my younger days in Grangetown. One was an old school pal and the other was someone I used train with at the gym when we were teenagers. I didn't try to hide the fact I knew them. I had the attitude that if others didn't like me talking to them, they should speak to me about it or mind their own business. I had no patience for the petty squabbles or the childish antics that went on around me. Sometimes it was like being amongst a load of kids who had never grown up. It was always the short termers who disrupted prison life and it's the persistent offenders who are supported by the Rehabilitation of Offenders Act (ROA).

Such offenders get a continual string of short sentences. However many sentences they get, their convictions eventually become spent. When a conviction becomes spent, it means that legally, they are no longer required to disclose them at job interviews. Those who serve longer than four years imprisonment, never have their convictions spent.

The government agrees that longer termers are the least likely to re-offend yet they have these ludicrous rules that longer termers can never have a clean sheet. While I was in prison, I decided to study the environment that surrounded me. Word got around that I was studying psychology and one day, I was approached by the prison social worker who asked if I would like to be become a 'listener'. The prison ran a listener service where prisoners were able to talk to other prisoners about their problems. It was like a counselling service but only to listen, not give out advice. I started to get the bug for analysing and researching. I also took up long distance learning, gaining diplomas in psychology, criminology and psychology, child psychology and counselling theory, through a private learning provider called The National Home Study College.

Sadly, years later, I discovered that all the certificates I was so proud of, were worthless. The college was under investigation for issuing certificates that were not officially recognised. It didn't faze me though because by then I had gained two genuine degrees. It did make me think though, that criminals could be found anywhere, even in education. My family helped pay for my materials from a company that turned out to be a scam. Even offenders can be victims of crime. Too many offenders lack empathy for their victims. They are so convinced they are the victims themselves, they blame everyone but themselves for their incarceration. Many blame their upbringing, society, their victims, the police for locking them up and the prison staff for keeping them in prison. While I was serving my sentence, although I could see this selfish trait in others, I couldn't see it in myself, but it was there. Years after my release, the penny finally dropped and I started to learn empathy towards those I had hurt in the past.

The prison grapevine was the first social network I had ever witnessed with its Chinese whispers, hearsay and false rumours. It was the fastest form of communication I had ever seen and it created all the same problems that today's social networks do. An incident could happen on one block and everyone would know about it on the next block within a blink of an eye. Considering most of the prison population is supposed to consist of poor communicators in the real world, they were superb communicators inside their own little world. They had their own form of language too that only they understood. They tapped on pipes to make themselves heard and passed things from one cell to another using small containers on the end of string. If they wanted to pass something to the cell next door, they swung it using enough string for the other person to catch it with their outstretched arms through the bars.

This would have been impossible in Durham prison because the windows were too high up and the bars were too close to each other to fit an arm through. There was more distance between cells in Durham too. It was hard enough getting some crumbs out of the window to feed the Pigeons.

The prison grapevine caused fights, rifts, paranoia and stress. The short termers on six to 18 month sentences who ran around popping pills and being a nuisance were the biggest threats. They struggled with spending time inside, despite serving the shortest sentences. I would often hear them asking one another for 'temys', or temegesic tablets, which are painkillers. I never touched any kind of drugs in prison and was once asked how I was able to do my sentence with a 'straight head'. This was one of the biggest changes I noticed during my second time in prison. Many of the prisoners were incapable of doing their time and a lot couldn't do it without drugs. They couldn't see a single day through without some form of sedative. One of the worst kind of criminals were the white collar criminals such as solicitors, doctors, business men and professionals. They were deemed to be better suited for the easier life and regime of the open prison because of their social standing. They hid behind the system and their own superiority. Not only did they regard themselves as superior to the rest of us, but so did the criminal justice system which protected them due their higher class status in the upper echelons of British society. This is a side of Britishness I find despicable beyond words. A lot of white collar criminals had elderly and vulnerable victims and in many cases, not just one, but hundreds. Had these people mugged an old lady, they would have been beaten within an inch of their lives inside prison.

Why is it deemed more acceptable for the white collar criminal to scam the elderly from their life savings than a street thug to mug an elderly person? It seems that physical injury is regarded as something far worse than mental and emotional injury, yet psychological scars can often have far greater consequences for victims.

Back in the early days in Durham prison, although the prison regime was stricter and the building was grim, dirty and old, prisoners seemed more stable and stronger. The biggest change, was the dominant drug problem now in prisons. In the early days, there would be the occasional nicking after a random cell or body strip search revealed some hidden cannabis, or one of the night watch screws had caught a whiff of weed wafting from underneath someone's cell door the night before and reported it. However, more than 10 years on, I could see that things had changed and there was a huge drug problem now which was directly associated to other kinds of problems such as violence. Much harder drugs were now being used such as heroin and cocaine. Syringes were also being smuggled in with some visitors using their own children as a way to get drugs through on visits. Another culture shock was the change I saw in the the inmate culture and regime. The British archetypal prison officer had long gone. The screws no longer strutted around in their immaculate uniforms, gleaming boots and medal ribbons displayed on their tunics from their military service. The former military style prison officer had been replaced by casually dressed, liberal thinking screws. Many of them had no military background, unlike their predecessors.

In the old system, prisoners knew their boundaries whereas now, prisoners showed no respect for themselves, authority, or their fellow inmates, and would use violence under the slightest provocation. The younger prisoners were also very different to the young prisoner culture I had once been part of. They no longer kept their heads down, fell in with the rules of the prison, or respected the experienced old lag inmates, as we had. They rebelled against everything and lacked mental strength and maturity. There was also another major change. Female screws working on the landings. There was sometimes one or two working in workshops in the past, but never on actual landings, locking and unlocking male inmates. Some had real power trip agendas, but I had always been a sucker for a pretty face and I liked them being around.

We called them 'screwesses' and I couldn't imagine them working with the old school, chauvinist male screws from back in the day. These were modern, independent women, who we addressed as 'Miss', while male screws were addressed as 'Boss'. In Young Prisoner institutions, screws were called 'Sir', and it was best not to be caught calling them 'screw'.

A glimpse of my favourite female screw working on the landing could brighten my day. I never had an issue with any of the female officers; some were like a breath of fresh air. Having female officers working directly with male prisoners balanced the ethos of everyday prison life. Some of the more foolish inmates would verbally abuse or harass them. One lady told me that an inmate shouted to her to "show us your cat!". Female screws were sexually discriminated against on a daily basis, and although I can't say for sure, I believe they had prejudice from some of their male colleagues too. The downside of introducing female screws to the landings had other problems too. Love affairs happened, and though I knew of some who had affairs with teachers, I didn't know anyone personally who had an affair with a female officer. The only personal experience I can relate to around this subject, was when I was released, I kept in touch with one of my teachers. Also while I was studying on the education department, one of the teachers was pulled aside and given a talking to for being too familiar with me.

Women had a different approach because women don't need to flex their muscles and have their ego stroked as men do. I have found this with police women too. I was always able to converse with women much easier than men, but some offenders felt intimidated by women. Some particularly hated being confronted by female officers. Ethnicity had also become a part of the new prison culture and I can remember when a French prisoner was brought on the landing. He was abused and ridiculed as he desperately tried to become accepted by acting the clown, but this just made him an even bigger target. I remember talking to him when he first came in. He seemed a normal looking young man with a head of thick, curly, black hair, who just wanted to blend in with the crowd. By the time the others had finished with him, he had shaved his head with a Bic razor and his behaviour had changed so drastically, he was removed from the wing, never to be seen by any of us again. He would do things to make the others laugh and bring attention to himself.

The wing was run by a North East crime godfather of ethnic origin. Samuel was an imposing figure of massive build and about six feet- four. He was dark skinned, had a shaven head and very piercing, yet not menacing eyes. He was charismatic with a lot of presence, but he never threw his weight around. The screws got on well with him. First thing every morning, he was unlocked before anyone else and last thing at night, locked up after everyone else. One of his mates ran a bath for him every evening after we were all locked up for the night, and when we all went to the gym in the morning, he would be there before any of us. At lunch time, where we were all rationed to four slices of bread, he was handed a full loaf. The first time I walked into his cell, I was surprised to see a mass of clothes hanging on coat hangers that he wore for court appearances and visits. It was obvious the screws liked to keep him happy because he kept a lid on things. In other words, if there were any problems or skirmishes on the wing, he could sort it out. It kind of reminded me of the sitcom, Porridge and the character, Harry Grout who was the prison godfather. I had only seen this sort of thing on television, but now it was reality. I made no attempt to befriend him but he seemed quite cheerful and witty. He was originally from Nigeria, and had been made to fight in the Biafran war at a very young age. He had settled in Newcastle as a young man, so he had Geordie accent. One day he approached me and introduced himself, and asked if I was expecting a life sentence. I was surprised at this remark, so I asked why he said it. He told me it was because I went about my business the way lifers do. What he meant was, I acted sensibly, didn't act the clown and just got on with my time. This is simply known as getting your head down and doing your 'bird'.

His observation of me was later proved correct too when I would spend the rest of my sentence with lifers, developing a bond and mutual respect with them. I found I had lots in common with lifers. I had a mutual interest in education and writing with many of them. I could also understand how so many of them had ended up in their predicament. I could relate to how they had bottled things up and finally exploding. I had almost ended up being one of them. I eventually conducted my own study of the lifers I got to know the closest.

The more I got to know Samuel, the more I was fascinated by him. His fearsome reputation was projected by the hangers-on and the young people in awe of him, but he was much more than just a hard man. He was a highly intellectual man who had lived a life full of tragic experiences. I remained in touch with him after I was released from prison and got to know his family quite well. Samuel finally went to trial and was sentenced to two and a half years. He had actually spent a total of two and a half years on remand waiting to be sentenced. There had been delays throughout the trial such as when one of the witnesses had a heart attack while giving evidence against Samuel. Such was the fear he instilled. Therefore, for the time he had already spent in prison, he walked free. He had spent the longest time on remand than any other prisoner in the UK. I later met up with him in Newcastle, but didn't see him very often. The last I saw of him, he was at Leeds Crown Court on trial for attempted murder after shooting someone over a debt. He was handed a life sentence with a strange tariff of four years.

Prison was full of characters and everyone had a story to tell. One of my fellow inmates, Jack had been remanded for an armed robbery. He had served 12 years in an American Penitentiary. He had the presence of a man who wasn't to be messed with. He had long hair and was covered in tattoos. He kept to himself and no one bothered him. He wasn't very tall and not large built, but he had soul and the heart of a lion.

There was a bit of rival tension between those from Sunderland and Newcastle which stemmed from a lifetime feud between the two cities. Sometimes, they would hurl insults at one another.

AIDS had also become a problem in prison over recent years. As I observed all the cultural changes around me, I thought back to a talk we were once given in Low Newton about a new epidemic attacking the UK called AIDS. We were told how we must be careful not to share our drinking mugs and eating utensils with other inmates. More than 10 years on, AIDS had become a problem in prisons. Fortunately there was a lot more knowledge about it compared to when it was in its infancy back in the 1980's.

Changes with regards privileges included the installation of plug sockets in our cells for radios whereas in the 80's, we could only use battery operated radios. When our batteries ran out, we would chew them as it made them last a bit longer, or at least until pay day. There were light switches inside the cells so we could turn our own lights out whenever we pleased, as opposed to them being outside the cells and being plunged into darkness at exactly 10:00pm each night. We had a toilet and wash basin in our cells instead of the old plastic chamber pots and bowls. Pay phones were now available for prisoners at the end of each landing as opposed to the regulation two letters a week we were once allowed to send and receive. Knife attacks had also become a common occurrence in prison and attacks were usually over debt. Also, because of the new drugs culture that had entered our prisons, random drug testing, MDT (Mandatory Drug Testing), was introduced during my sentence in 1996. The rationale for MDT was to deter the use of drugs within prison; to identify those to treat and those to punish. All prisoners are subject to the random testing programme and prisons are required to test five to 10 percent of their population each month. Refusal by a prisoner to be tested could lead to up to 28 days loss of remission. The urine tests are sent outside the prison for testing to a central laboratory. A positive result means that the prisoners are sent for adjudication. This usually results in loss of privileges and remission - 14 days for cannabis, 21 for opiates. Prisoners are taken from their workplaces and cells at random to give urine samples. Two screws take the prisoner to the medical officer who gives them a container for a urine sample. Results of the test are given to the prisoner in a note under the cell door a few days later.

Softer drugs such as cannabis remain in a person's system for 28 days, thus increasing a prisoner's risk of being tested positive. MDT's were always carried out on a weekday. Therefore, to avoid testing positive after a weekend of non-stop drug use, prisoners could use the hard stuff and be clear by Monday morning.

In prison, I developed an awareness of who to associate with and who to stay clear of. The nastier inmates were like Vultures. They would hover around waiting for opportunities to 'tax', or demand goods from any new vulnerable prisoner who was an easy target. In other words, bully him into handing over whatever they wanted from him. One day, someone came in for the first time and was taxed for his watch and other belongings. It was rife, but the cowards who took part in this sort of activity, only chose the weakest inmates.

Weakness is something inmates can never show in prison. One of my cellmates, Steve, was seen crying several times and his life was made hell from then on. He had shown weakness so he became a target for many months to come. The brutality changed him as it does for many who experience the grim realities of prison life. Several months after I was sentenced, I saw Steve again. He had changed from the energetic and often, upbeat person, to one who was withdrawn, pale, and oppressed.

Six months passed and my trial day had finally arrived. It was 15th December 1995 and I had decided to plead guilty, so there was no need for a trial. This meant the judiciary were spared the expense of bringing in a jury for which I would be credited. I had been going back and forth to crown court for several months when I entered my plea and court reports were requested. Judge Peter Fox decided that as I was pleading guilty anyway, a lesser charge of 'wounding with intent' (section 18) should be entered as opposed to attempted murder which the Crown Prosecution Service (CPS) was trying to impose. He set a trial date there and then so now the day of sentencing had arrived. The usual process took place with the journey to court in a sweat box; the long hours in the cells beneath the courts and the odd cup of tea and a bacon butty.

I wanted to take every opportunity to save myself from a lengthy stretch, so prior to my sentencing date, I had taken the advice from a fellow prisoner to write a letter to the judge offering my own mitigating circumstances. Using my best hand writing, I filled two sides of A4 paper explaining in depth, how I had allowed my emotions to get the better of me which had led to my predicament. I also described how I intended to use my time in prison to educate myself as a way of opening doors to a better future. Just before sentence was passed, the court usher handed my letter to the judge and as he respectfully read every word to himself, the courtroom fell silent. After reading it, he looked across to me and told me to stand up. He then said to me: "You have explained to me your actions today better than anyone else has been able to in this court. You said, you allowed your emotions to get the better of you and that is what you did. I commend you on your attempt to educate yourself while being on remand and with the sentence I hand out today, you can use that time to study. I sentence you to five years."

As my sentence was passed, I felt that the judge's words were very sincere. I set my sights on achieving great things in the world of academe. Later, I found out that the judge was ready to give me a much longer sentence, but changed his mind after reading my letter. It was then that I really learned the power of the written word.

I was taken back to Holme House after I had been sentenced and my personal clothes I had been allowed to wear while on remand were exchanged for dark blue prison clothing which matched the mood of my new allocation on the 'dark side'. After the usual reception process, I was taken to C Wing and although only yards from where I had just spent the last six months, it was a total contrast. Now I understood why they called it the dark side and why my fellow inmates used to tell me to make the most of my time on remand. They were always warning me that it would be completely different once convicted.

Those words were ringing in my ears as I was escorted to my new landing. Several inmates were hanging around outside their cell doors. I was immediately aware that they were weighing me up. As I walked along, I became aware that my physique stood out as the two heavy bags I was carrying made my neck and shoulder muscles bulge. A muscular physique can do two things. It can keep people away and it can attract those who want to prove their masculinity and challenge you. Challenging one another in the gym is the healthiest way to do this because if the next man is lifting more, it is motivation to work harder. This is healthy competitiveness, albeit motivated by the escalating male ego. Some, however, felt that in order to make their mark, they had to intimidate or pick fights. Prisoners would size one another up as in the animal kingdom.

I was lucky to have a good cell mate on the dark side, but I didn't like many of the others. I had made a few friends on A2 remand wing and it was a place where every day was different. Everyone was eagerly waiting to be sentenced. Some were optimistic of what to expect at court which kept them going. Some of the older, more experienced inmates would relish in offering the lesser experienced advice. Some were bitterly disappointed when they got longer sentences than they had expected while others walked free. Everyone would be taking an interest in each other's trials waiting to hear what sentences had been handed down and who had been acquitted.

From the day someone is remanded, there are several trips to and from court for plea entry, directions and for trial dates to be set. It is lengthy and laborious, but inmates are generally glad to break the monotony of daily routine and to get away from the prison for the day.

Before my case was transferred to Crown Court I had to make several trips to and from Guisborough Magistrates Court. Each time we were taken to court, we had to pack all our belongings in polythene bags the night before ready to take with us in case we were granted bail. The next morning, we were unlocked from our cells early and given breakfast before everyone else. We were then taken down to reception and locked inside the large holding cell where we would wait anxiously to get the pre court processing out of the way. There would be a screw on reception doing all the paperwork, and one standing just outside our door. Every 10 minutes or so, he would summon five or six prisoners at a time. We were searched then handed a box containing our clothes we came to prison wearing; or a set of clothes brought in by our visitors to wear for court. They would then get us to sign for our property once it had been inspected for contraband. We were then herded back into the holding cell until they were ready to take us to court at which point they would unlock the door and read a list of names and the courts we were attending including Teesside, Newcastle, and Sunderland. Each prisoner was handcuffed to one another in twos then taken to the vans waiting outside.

Whenever it was my turn to be processed, my name was called out individually as I was the only one going to Guisborough Magistrates Court.

One day I was abruptly searched and ordered to go and get changed. The screw who searched me was particularly rude towards me that morning. Once I had been searched and changed into my clothes, he then escorted me to the sex offender holding cell. I stopped dead in my tracks and said: "I'm not a sex offender, boss!" I realised what his problem was now.

"What are you charged with?" he said.

I told him that it was attempted murder. He had thought that because I was being processed alone, that I was a vulnerable prisoner. He'd not been told that I was the only prisoner appearing at Guisborough and had a taxi waiting. He took me back to the holding cell where the others were waiting. One of the lads asked why I'd been taken to the sex offenders' cell - nothing goes unnoticed in prison. If I hadn't known that the cell was for sex offenders, I could have been in danger from other prisoners and oblivious to it until it was too late.

Monotony is the thing I found the hardest to deal with in prison. The days were so long and boring. Even a cell search would break this monotony. The screws that did cell searches were nicknamed, 'burglars' by inmates. They would turn up with a Spaniel sniffer dog and go through every inch of the cell; take all the bedding apart and rummage through clothing and personal belongings.

I hated my new surroundings and was already wishing that I was back on the remand wing. Some of the other prisoners had bad attitudes and would congregate in their own little cliques. They all used to hang out during association in the upstairs television room and inhale cannabis through a homemade bong which was a plastic bottle with a pipe pushed through a hole in the side of it. They would sit there inhaling as much as they could and behaving like infants. Their giggling and pathetic banter grinded on me. Christmas in Holme House was mind numbing to say the least. There was an ugly looking Christmas tree at the end of the landing; festive tunes serenading from radios and an attempt by the kitchen staff to offer Christmas dinner of sorts. I'd just been sentenced, so I was re-categorised to category C status then given two choices of where I wanted to be transferred to in the New Year. My choices were to either remain at Holme House or go to Acklington Prison in Northumberland. I had to be interviewed by the senior officer for my transfer who pointed out that because I was charged with attempted murder, I was a failure. I retorted that at least I wasn't a screw. There were one or two screws who tried to be funny with snide remarks like this which to me only highlighted their ignorance and made them look stupid.

Despite some of the screws' bad attitudes and the infantile behaviour of the inmates on C wing, I started my sentence with a great sense of relief. Judge Fox's words gave me massive encouragement. I had crafted my writing so well, that I was even able to reduce my own sentence with my prose. But I had meant every word and was able to prove it years later.

In my remaining weeks at Holme House, I was told horror stories of Acklington, so asked if I could change my choice of transfer. My request was refused and on January 3rd 1996, I was sent to HMP Acklington.

18. Doing Time with Lifers

Before being transferred to the lifer wing [E unit], I had been inducted and allocated a cell on D Unit. My first diary entry read: "I'm going to stay behind my door for the next three years." I felt anxious and paranoid. I felt uncomfortable mingling on the landings of D Unit. The gangs of short termers made everyone's lives a misery; prison was just a game to them. Three days later I was scheduled to be transferred to E Unit where the lifers were housed. It was much more stable there. Who in the general public would understand this? In their minds the worst criminals are those who kill, but if they were to spend a week inside a prison, they would soon prefer to be in the company of convicted killers to petty criminals. This is a generalisation as it depends on the individual, but these lifers were first and only time offenders. They didn't share the same erratic behaviour patterns as the short termers and persistent offenders.

Once on E Unit, I felt an immediate sense of calm. Being on D Unit had been like being back in a psychiatric hospital. At least in hospital the patients were all on prescribed medication. On D Unit, they were self-medicating, popping all sorts of pills (mainly temgesic as mentioned earlier), just to get through their days. Drug taking and pill popping was the scourge of prison life. I could have a normal conversation with someone one day, then next time they would be different and perhaps even aggressive towards me. On E Unit, even my cell had a calming effect on me. It was dark where the last occupant had covered the window with a thin bed cover. The hot steel pipe made it warm and cosy - or at least as cosy as a cell could be. It needed a good paint, but I felt I could serve my time there and not feel intimidated by the crazy activity around the landings. The peacefulness was only occasionally disrupted by other fixed term prisoners who unfortunately were also allowed to reside on E Unit. Drugs were rife, but apart from some cannabis smoking, lifers didn't partake generally in this sort of activity. It wasn't worth the risk.

Some of the lifers in Acklington were de-categorised and spent the remainder of their sentences in open prisons. Some were kept as category C prisoners for longer, until they were deemed suitable for open conditions. Some had already previously been released on licence but later recalled and returned to prison for not adhering to the conditions of their licences.

Released lifers are subject to life licence which remains in force for the duration of their natural life. They may be recalled to prison at any time to continue serving their sentence in prison if they are considered high risk. Therefore, they don't need to commit another crime to be sent back to prison. They don't need to go back to court or be questioned by police. A mere sign that a lifer is going back to their old ways is enough to have them returned to prison. For example, old triggers such as drink and drugs must be avoided and behaviour must be exemplary. So for lifers on licence, they must do all they can to change old behaviours and habits to stay out of prison. One of the lifers I knew had been recalled from a hostel where he continually breached the rules by being drunk on the premises. He was returned to Acklington Prison and had been there several years by the time I left.

As for the lifers in Acklington, it was clear to me that some would have been better suited in psychiatric hospitals, although not a psychologist, or psychiatrist, I knew the signs. It was evident from the outset that they had a lot to tell and that no one else had ever really listened to them before. By now I was a budding criminologist with ambitions to become a successful academic. I was already immersed within my laboratory with as many participants as were willing to take part.

I continued to look for willing participants who I felt comfortable enough with and who felt equally comfortable with me enough to delve into the darkest corners of their minds. I wanted to find out about their lives but first I had to gain their trust. I was the same age as most of them and I had committed the same offence as most of them too but I was luckier than all of them because my victim had survived. I set about choosing my friends very carefully by getting to know them over several months. Had I gone head first into trying to get inside their heads, it could have had catastrophic consequences. It would take me a lot longer to befriend some than others. There seemed to be a lot of back biting and prison grapevine gossip between the lifers too. Prison had made some of them very bitter and angry over the years with the systems rules and regulations, including the breakdown of marriages and estranged relationships with their children, siblings and parents.

I knew my personality would clash with those who blamed everything and everyone but themselves, so I avoided them. I became friends with a Geordie lad called Paul. His heart was in the right place, he used to tell people I was an author. I liked the fact that he looked up to me. I could use this to gain his trust and get introduced to other lifers through him. He was eight years into a life sentence for murder, but wouldn't reveal enough for me to be able to ask him questions about his crime. Two days later, Paul brought Mark to my cell. I had seen him around as he was situated on the same landing as me in the end cell. He was about five foot three inches tall, portly, had severe eczema and bodily hygiene problems.

He never spoke to anyone, I had looked through his spy hole several times to see him always standing and staring out through the bars of his cell window. Mark revealed to me he was a paranoid schizophrenic. "They won't move me to a hospital," he said. I sensed an extremely disturbed character beneath the surface. I felt too uneasy in his presence, so I took it no further. My instincts were correct because six months later, the prison staff were forced to hospitalise him. He boiled over and went into a major meltdown, smashing everything in his cell. It must have taken the whole unit staff to restrain and move him to the hospital wing.
How many more are like this?
How many more ticking time bombs are in prison just waiting to explode?

Paul, on the other hand, got his comeuppance when it was discovered that his murder victim had been a disabled person. Dennis Stafford, a former associate of the Kray and Richardson gang, exposed him after obtaining disc files from his trustee job in the Governor's office.

Dennis was the highest profile lifer I became acquainted with during my time in prison, but I doubted very much that I would manage to get inside his head. He was famously jailed for the One Armed murder, the cold blooded gangland execution that inspired the Michael Caine thriller *Get Carter*. It involved East End villain Stafford, who claimed that he and a friend, Michael Luvaglio, were framed for the shooting of fellow gangster, Angus Sibbet in January 1967. The case was one of the most notorious killings in the North East, and the first gangland killing, sparking fears that organised crime was gaining a foothold in the North East. Luvaglio's Italian surname sparked the headline, 'The Mafia are coming.' The trial was also one of the biggest seen in the North East. During my time in Acklington, I spoke to Dennis many times and got the impression he was somewhat aloof to the rest. When I asked him about the Krays, he told me they were illiterates. He was unpopular amongst other lifers who felt he had special privileges. He was the only prisoner with a computer in his cell at a time when computers were still fairly new. He said it because he had arthritis in his fingers, so found it difficult pressing down the keys on a typewriter. One day, through sheer jealousy, someone smashed it up after Dennis had left his cell door open when he went for shower. I could see he was getting special treatment. One day, he proudly showed me his identification badge, with his new job title working as an administrator in the Governor's office. Stafford was later transferred to Ford open prison – the elite open jail of open jails. His autobiography *Fun Loving Criminal* was published in 2007.

Simon was 11 years into his life sentence and it was hard to believe he was even in prison. Small and slim in stature with a good head of curly hair and softly spoken, he didn't fit the mould of what is perceived as a criminal type. He came across as a gentle natured person and was very well educated. He was studying for a degree through the Open University. We talked about education a lot and the emotional effects of being in prison. He thought that doing time was more difficult if a person was intelligent. I felt he had a point. He told me that one day he banged on his ceiling because the prisoner above him was playing his music too loud who then stormed down to Simon's cell and blacked his eye, Simon didn't retaliate.

Simon explained the devastating consequences that getting into trouble can have on a lifer's sentence. I was beginning to realise that they constantly walked on eggshells. I also knew that I could never have lived that kind of existence.

Lifers who tried to buck the system were not only risking their freedom, but were looked down on by their fellow lifers. This was a contrast to fixed termers who revelled in trying to beat the system. However, as many others over the years have learned the hard way, this is an impossible task. One prison officer pointed out to me one day, that lifers always screw up at the last hurdle. He was referring to one who absconded from Wealstun with only months to serve after having already served most of his sentence.

I had to be careful of who I wrote about for the sake of both parties. It had to be strictly confidential. I met Ben, a handsome fellow with long, curly, black hair. He had a pleasant smile and was very approachable, but rather quiet. His wife had moved in with his best friend once Ben had been incarcerated, yet despite being bitter, was still loyal and trustworthy. Sometimes, he was too quiet and withdrawn to the point of it being nauseating. I often got frustrated at him and felt as though I wanted to shake him. This was because we were close friends and shared a bond. He admitted to me that he killed because he bottled his emotions and allowed them to fester. He had since done an assertiveness course in prison to help him learn to let things go and to talk about his emotions. I understood this perfectly because I had often been in the same boat myself. Courses such as Ben's assertiveness course are often criticised as being a box ticking exercise and a way of keeping prisoners under control, but such courses can benefit prisoners. Aside from the mental benefits, they also give prisoners chances to keep their privileges and will often help them to be considered for parole.

I wondered if repressed emotions were a common trait amongst violent offenders. Men are not great communicators at the best of times and I was aware that there was a huge problem with communication skills amongst offenders.

I found though that one of the most interesting things about lifers was that they were all, in their own way, very ordinary people. This reinforced the idea that there isn't a type of person to end up in prison and that anyone can one day find themselves serving life for murder or manslaughter.

It was this ordinariness of the prisoners that became the most critical part of my observations. None of the lifers I got to know most intimately were career criminals, persistent offenders or even bad people beneath the surface.

Mike and another lifer called Les both could have been charged with manslaughter and been released years earlier. In the heat of a moment, people threaten to kill one another without thinking about any possible consequences. How many times do we flippantly say: 'I'll kill you!'?. Mike had been overheard saying this to his victim three weeks before shooting him in the arm with a double barrel shotgun. He told me it was his intention to just wound him which he did, but later his victim died from his injuries. I couldn't help but wonder if he was trying to fool himself or me. Perhaps he was in denial, but he didn't need to fool me; he was going home in a few weeks' time. Lifers were continually subjected to regular, thorough psychological assessments before they were allowed to be released back into society. To show signs of denial or lack of remorse was enough to delay their release. I believed him as he seemed a completely together, confident, and assertive person. In fact, he was so unlike a lot of the others, he was shunned by them and accused of being a 'grass'. I never believed this. Although Mike deliberately caused the injuries to the victim, he would have still been a suspect, due to his threat; even if he wasn't personally responsible.

One day, I was arguing with Les in my cell. Someone had been talking about me behind my back and I was thinking of confronting him about it when I saw him. Les was furious. He was practically shouting at me to try and settle things without violence. He wanted me to talk or shake hands and make it up. I thought that this would be a sign of weakness, until Les revealed that a man had once knocked his drink over at a pub and a fight ensued. The man was killed when Les delivered his final punch knocking the man to the ground where he hit his head. This made me wonder why Les wasn't serving a manslaughter charge rather than murder, but I didn't press him.

It just shows that the smallest incident such as a weekend brawl could result in someone's death. Every lifer's story could have easily been my own or anyone else's. Every person takes freedom for granted, but it can so easily change. Lives can be lost and those responsible lose their freedom causing permanent emotional and psychological damage for everyone's families.

It soon occurred to me that one of the most outstanding differences between lifers and the rest of the prison population was their appearances. None of them gave an aura of aggression, looked thuggish, or acted tough. Most fixed termers tried to give off a persona as being hard, so no one would mess with them. They would muscle up in the gym, shave their heads and swagger along the landings. None of the lifers possessed any of these traits. I began to realise why their self-image was so important to them. They were mentally preparing for their release so had set about adopting a new identity with a clean cut image. I first noticed Mike one Saturday afternoon in the television room unlocking and entering a small cupboard area in the corner. He was loading a video for the scheduled movie showing. He was a handsome man, physically fit, very clean cut and well groomed. One day, we were lying on our beds watching television and talking when I told him that I thought he was a member of staff when I first saw him. He took this as a compliment. After years of incarceration it was important to some of the lifers that their identity be transformed to the point of being more like their jailers than their fellow inmates.

Mike told me that he didn't want to look like a criminal and went to a lot of trouble to avoid this image. He never shaved his head nor muscled up in the gym. I found it ironic that a prisoner serving life for murder shared society's views of what criminals look like. He told me that when he was released, he wanted to reintegrate into society, quietly, blending in with his new wife and with no stigma attached. He was genuine and determined to be accepted by others and become a respectable, family man. Establishing the right impression was essential to him. It was a major, personal transition from his prisoner identity, to that of a married, family man. This has been well researched by desistance scholars whereby a small number of factors are sturdy correlates of desistance from crime. For example, good marriages, stable work, transformation of identity, and aging. The processes of desistance from crime and other forms of problem behaviour appear to be similar.

Clothing was also an identity statement for prisoners. In Wealstun, we wore our own clothes. Many of the inmates would go to great lengths to wear particular labelled clothing as a way of displaying their individualism and wealth. Displaying a wealthy image was a competitive business for some prisoners as each tried to outdo the other. They were making a statement about their success in the outside world. Mike was certainly no exception either, but for him, being smartly dressed in his own clothes made him feel less of a prisoner.

Lifers nearing the end of their term in open prisons were allowed regular home leave. They were allowed to spend five days at a time at home with their families. They were also allowed community visits where they could spend up to six hours outside the prison with family and friends. Sometimes the worry, strain and frustration of not being able to deal with family crises as they arose would cause some to abscond. For some lifers, alternating their lifestyle while on leave, while also residing in prison was just too much to deal with. Some were just allured by other things such as one prisoner who with only three months remaining of his 17 years, absconded. He had been working outside the prison at a local café and the allure of a sexy waitress was too much to resist. They ran away together eloping somewhere far away. I was sure that it couldn't have lasted. I can't imagine a life of always looking over my shoulder, wondering when I was going to be caught. When in prison, lifers don't have a release date, just a tariff. This is an approximate length of time they must serve before being considered for parole, but as I said earlier, they can be hauled back to jail for as long as the authorities seek fit. A lifer being caught on the run can expect a lengthy stay in secure conditions which is a far cry from the open prisons they've become accustomed to.

Friendships could also be tested at times. One day in Acklington, Ben was brutally assaulted by his friend, Sean, over nothing more than an innocuous remark. Like most offenders, Sean blamed anything but himself, while a friend of Sean's blamed the Dunblane massacre that had recently happened. According to him this had disturbed Sean as he was a father. I thought this was a ridiculous thing to say. There were plenty of prisoners with children who hadn't attacked anyone. They were mainly broken men with amputated spirits. Most had lost families, wives, and children who had either disowned them or died. John was an example of this. He had been sent to prison as part of a biker's pact despite being innocent. While serving his 10 years he lost his wife to cancer. When he was released, he lived another few weeks having contracted the disease himself.

Other lifers who I was acquainted with, but didn't know well, included one of the most detestable lifers I had the displeasure to meet. He was a short stout, arrogant, Italian who had chopped his wife's head off which he'd kept in a carrier bag on the passenger seat of his car for days. He was one of those I gave a wide berth to. Another was a former prison officer, I mentioned earlier, who had decapitated his wife. I wouldn't have imagined that he would ever have had so much as a parking fine.

Another man was serving life for a religious killing. He was a Sikh who used the name Peter. Myself and some of the other lads called him 'The Turbanator'. Sikhs have a ceremonial sword, or Kirpan, as part of their five K's (articles of faith). Peter took his sword to a family member severing his head. When I met him, he was eight years into a life tariff and was unwilling to disclose any more about his crime. He was a jolly man and had a clean cut image, which made it difficult for me to think of him as a murderer. I felt that none of these men would ever see the inside of a prison again. Of all the lifers I studied, none ever showed any signs of aggression toward myself or other prisoners. They were not typically violent criminals, despite having committed murder. This period of my life was the most eye opening seeing how imprisonment had changed these men forever and also the biggest deterrent of crime.

Unfortunately for me, my mental health issues prevented me from following a steady path in life especially as my personality disorder reached its peak after I was released from prison. Several years later, I looked back on my time with the lifers, and how their words of wisdom had a great impact on me.

Mike was released after serving 13 years and was looking forward to starting a new life with his new wife, Sarah. She was a lovely person. I met her several times on visits and later, outside. They looked very much in love and I hoped they would be very happy. I kept in touch with Mike until I left Newcastle. The last I heard, he and Sarah were happily married and he had even learned to drive at the age of 45. I didn't hear from Ben again but heard that he'd been released. I didn't hear from any of the others either, they had all tried to move on with their lives in one way or another. I passed my Open University Social Sciences course in 1997 and was offered a place at Northumbria University to study Criminology. In February 1998, I was released and several months later, enrolled on my degree course in September that year. This was the biggest break I had ever had, so there was no going back. Although my lifer friends had opened my eyes and given me a snap shot of what I could become if I didn't change my ways, it would be several years before I could really turn things around. It is very rare to be able to have a snap shot of your own future. We can all imagine how we may turn out, but the unique factor here, was that I was looking at mine through the eyes of people I shared identical behavioural patterns with. Several months after leaving prison while I was studying at university, I read one the most inspirational books I'd ever read called, *Psychological Survival: The Experience of Long-term Imprisonment* by Laurie Taylor and Stan Cohen. The publication of the book came about after sociologist, Laurie Taylor, took the unusual step of starting sociology classes in the maximum security E Wing of Durham Prison. Some of its residents included John McVicar though not for long, as McVicar tunnelled his way out soon after the classes began. The formal boundaries between teacher and learner were blurred within weeks, and the classes soon developed into unplanned discussions and then into an extraordinary research project. The second edition, published in 1981, includes a postscript by McVicar who by this stage had traded in his sawn off shotgun for a typewriter. Laurie Taylor's journey into Durham's E Wing and beyond, involved friend and colleague Stan Cohen, a sociologist at Durham University. The Cohen and Taylor collaboration continued for many years and resulted in several major publications inspired by the Durham Prison experience. This included the book *Escape Attempts: The Theory and Practice of Resistance to Everyday Life* (1976).

Although *Psychological Survival* was a text that one of my criminology lecturers had suggested, it meant more to me than just being another book on my reading list. As I got to know each lifer, it became more difficult to believe they had committed such terrible crimes. The fact that I had just managed to escape a life sentence for a vicious attack made it easier for me to be accepted by the lifers and for me to accept them too. They only associated with one another - rarely with fixed termers. It was a very close-knit circle and it took a lot for an outsider to be accepted. It was evident they regarded me as being almost one of them. I used the tools I had at hand to the best of my ability. I was already part of the environment with willing participants and some basic knowledge of research skills through my social sciences study and intense reading. As Cohen and Taylor had conducted their research while working as teachers in Durham Prison in the 1960's, I did mine as a serving prisoner. I continued my journey through higher education which had provided an escape from my damaging lifestyle. And since my entry into education 18 years ago, I have become acquainted with other offenders both male and female who have also successfully followed the same path as I have. From the two years, six months I spent with the lifers, I learned about the value of education and how it had enabled them to focus their minds over a long period of imprisonment. For me, education has opened new doors and enabled me to forge a new identity and become accepted within a new culture despite my past.

19. A Prison without Walls

Wealstun Open Prison had previously been used in World War II to produce ammunition for the army and RAF. Since then, it had been Rudgate Open Prison then later renamed Wealstun Open Prison. It was next door to what used to be Thorpe Arch Remand Centre where I was sent in 1983 as a young prisoner. Since then, Thorpe Arch had amalgamated with Rudgate to become HMP Wealstun, Open and Closed prisons. This was a historic development for the Prison Service and had the effect of creating a Category C (closed) side and Category D (open) side within one establishment. Wealstun's whole establishment approach was aimed at progressive transfer of suitable prisoners from the closed side to the open side. It was an exciting time to be made a category D prisoner, and I couldn't get to Wealstun fast enough. However, due to the prison transport arrangements, I had to spend three days back at Holme House Prison en route. They were a very long three days. We weren't allowed anything from our private property. After all, it would have been too much trouble for them to open a bag and hand us something. It was much easier for them to hold us in a bare cell which was akin to solitary confinement. I passed the hours amusing myself, reading, and writing. I managed to get one of the cleaners who was hanging around the landings chatting to prisoners through their doors to fetch me a pen and some paper. When in these situations, I soon learned how to appreciate the simple things in life. A pen and some paper made my days easier. I also requested to see the prison Chaplain who brought me books that had been written by former inmates who had turned their lives around through religion.

I never found religion myself but I respect those who had and drawn comfort for it enough to change their lives through their faith. Many other prisoners would mock those who were religious seeing it as a hidden agenda to get parole.

Once arriving at Wealstun, we were processed through the closed side. At one point, things started to look as though they were going to go wrong when I was pulled to one side. My records showed that I had made a suicide attempt 10 years earlier and that I had a history of depression. For a brief moment it looked as though my Category D status was going to be revoked and I would be kept at the closed side. To my great relief, I was told that I could go to the open side as long as I didn't try to hurt myself again.

A lot of the prisoners in the open side had been transferred from the closed side of Wealstun. If we misbehaved, one of the threats was to be sent to the closed side. Open prisons are a different prison experience - they consist of mainly white collar criminals. Years later, when I became a student of criminology, I learned that some of these white collar criminals had more victims than some of the most violent ones through health and safety negligence which often resulted in many deaths. The elderly were often victims of their scams and fraud, yet these criminals were rarely treated the same as everyone else. This was an example of their elitism in prison. The white collar prisoners included solicitors, doctors, businessmen, judges, and former police officers. Some of them thought and acted as though they were superior to the other prisoners. They were more educated and had more wealth which they more than happy to keep reminding us about. Whenever a former police officer came in to prison, they never stayed long. They were usually recognised by someone whose paths had crossed in the past and shipped out immediately. I remember this happening one day when a police officer was recognised in the dinner queue. Whispers circulated that a traffic bobby was amongst us and within minutes, he was escorted from the dining hall and shipped out to another prison. Prisoners saw the police as their enemies for putting them in prison, yet they were surrounded by individuals who had scammed and stolen from the elderly and innocent. There was a former police officer who I befriended, but he wasn't recognised, probably because he had left the police a long time before. I never told anyone else that I knew he was a former police officer because I knew it would put him in danger. Others within my circle of friends knew of his past, but also kept it to themselves.

While the elitism within the open prison was sickening, the regime was easier with more opportunities such as education and employment outside the prison. Prisoners regularly made Hooch - a disgusting homebrew. The process of making this awful beverage was organised with such precision, expertise and teamwork. The kitchen orderlies would supply all the ingredients such as juice from canned fruit cocktail, yeast, and leftover bread. All of this was then put into plastic containers and left in a dark, cool place for up to two weeks. In our case, this was underneath the Chapel altar. I sampled it once and that was enough for me but some drank it regularly.

There were also nightly fence drops where prisoners would sneak out of their dormitories in the pitch black to meet someone from outside the prison who would then hurl contraband over the fence to them. Each night the screws would sneak around in the darkness trying to catch them. Sometimes I could hear them sprinting after someone or running through the dormitory corridors to try and cut them off as they scarpered. One night, one of my pad mates met his girlfriend at the fence, sneaked out, had sex with her, and then sneaked back in undetected. During the night, every hour or so, the screws would come round to check on us by shining their torches in our faces while we were trying to sleep. They had to do regular checks because it was so easy to abscond as many did. One night, I arranged to abscond with one of my fellow inmates but it never came off. We thought better of it in the end.

We could wear our own clothes in Wealstun and some of the more affluent inmates made sure they wore only the best gear. The nearest equivalent to this in the closed prisons, was when inmates would pay someone with tailoring skills a phone card or tobacco to tailor their prison shirts so they could look their best for visits.

I started going to the Chapel a lot with Ben who I used to knock around with in Acklington. I don't know if I was trying to search for something or just enjoying another social activity - probably both. I even converted from being a Protestant to a Catholic with Dave as my witness. I enjoyed the friends I found in the Chapel and I enjoyed the activities we took part in - such as the services and the regular meetings. I even did a few bible readings for the Chaplain and sometimes we would meet groups of college students who would come to the prison to talk to us or put on a play for us. The Chapel orderly, Richard, was a fellow inmate and his job was to keep the Chapel clean and tidy and arrange services, and meetings. He also used to hide contraband Whiskey as well as his Hooch under the priest's altar. Things like this helped us through our sentences. We got a laugh out of it. It may sound a strange thing to say, but we did have a lot of laughs in prison. Laughter got us through the long days. Some of the screws hated to see us laughing. They preferred to see us suffering instead. There was a real mixture of staff. Some would encourage us to do well and some just did their jobs who were neither for nor against us. Then, there were those who were even more bitter than some of the prisoners who had spent years in prison. I learned that prisons can affect all who live and work in them over time.

In 1996, a new Governor was appointed. She was called Stacey Tasker, who was a young, up and coming prison Governor. She became immediately popular amongst the inmates. I think she ruffled a few feathers amongst the staff who were against changes. A lot seemed to disappear over to the closed side. Oddly enough, they were the same ones we had issues with too. One of the assistant Governors was arrested one day. She'd upset a lot prisoners over the years denying them privileges that would have helped them and their families. One prisoner had once requested a home visit to see his baby being born. This would have been easy for her to sanction because we were all Category D low risk prisoners. However, she refused and later, paraded her own newly born baby around the prison. They say that what goes around, comes around. Later that year, it was revealed that she had been fiddling expenses and was subsequently paid a visit by the police at the prison. Someone got hold of a newspaper cutting of the report and pinned it to the wall in the education block much to the anger of the staff.

Stacey Tasker was a breath of fresh air. The prison changed dramatically overnight with new incentives for prisoners, more privileges, understanding, and opportunities. I started my Open University Foundation course in January 1997 which if I passed, would get me into University once I was released. I was actually accepted on the OU course while I was in Acklington but I was in Wealstun when my course started. I also chose to go to the prison education classes on a full time basis. There was a price to pay for this though because some of the inmates went out to work in the community such as in schools, catering establishments, and shops, but because I had chosen education, I was unable to leave the grounds. This resulted in me being more restricted than most - apart from a few community visits that almost cost me my freedom. I barely left the prison for the 18 months I was there. I had restricted my own freedom for the price of an education but it was worth it in the end.

Wealstun didn't have cells, it had dormitories with four or five men sharing. We had our own keys to the doors and could come and go as we pleased. Outside, we could roam around freely and we didn't have to walk in circles like in the closed prisons. There was an element of trust. There was a painted white boundary line about 200 yards from the main gate. We could walk out of the prison if we wanted to, but the consequences included extra jail time and being returned to a more secure prison. Three times a day, a deafening siren would screech through the air. It was originally used for air raids when Wealstun was an ammunition site. When this happened, everyone had to go immediately to their dormitories. The screws would then count everyone. If anyone was missing, they conducted a search and if they couldn't find them, police helicopters were called out. There were many prisoners who I wished would abscond. Some prisoners would inform on others by slipping notes in the letter box where we posted our letters.

It seemed bizarre to me that after spending most of my childhood years living on RAF bases, I would end up living back on them as converted prisons such as Acklington and Wealstun. My father was actually stationed at Acklington when he was in the RAF. He said it was a dump then too. Wealstun Open prison was split into two units, north and south. I was on south unit sharing a dormitory with three others. It was a long way from the confinement of a cell I'd been used to. We had large windows with no bars and at the end of the corridor were two swing doors leading to several pay phones. Phone cards were £2 each and we could buy them from a van that came around a few times a week. Phone cards were the main currency in prison as opposed to tobacco in the early days.

There was a football field surrounded by a fence which I used to run around 30 times every day as part of my personal fitness routine. I felt free and could lose myself for half an hour each day. I lost more weight during that time than ever before or since. It was very therapeutic. I could also see the Leeds United training grounds and academy just outside. One of the team's former players from the 1960's, Willie Bell and his wife, Mary, were helping the prison Chaplaincy by visiting prisons to talk to inmates and according to the Chaplaincy, were very effective.

One day, a larger than life individual introduced himself to me in the corridor after I came back from a run. He struck up a conversation with me saying he was keen to get the right people in his dormitory. He didn't suffer fools and neither did I. His name was Brian Cockerill who was serving two years 30 months for driving offences. Several years later he had his autobiography published called *The Taxman*. He was one of the best cellmates I ever had and aside from his fearsome reputation, he showed kindness and a genuine care for those he trusted around him. I trained with him a couple of times at the gym but it was impossible to keep up. One day he asked me to hold the punch bag for him while he laid into it. After about four or five punches, I couldn't hold it any longer. It felt like someone was trying to punch a hole through me. He had phenomenal power. We had nicknames for each other based on a comic strip in the British comic *Viz*. Brian was 'Big Vern', a parody of London mobsters such as the Kray twins. The Big Vern character is a heavily built square jawed man with very short hair, sunglasses, a heavy car coat and grizzled look. My nickname was 'Psycho Derek'. We used these names all the way through our time together.

One day, I twisted my ankle in a hole on the field while out running. The walk from my dormitory to the cookhouse each meal time was agony. Big Vern carried my plate and cutlery for me, stopping every few yards while I caught up. We had some good 'crack' at times. I shared cells and dormitories with lots of characters over my time in prison. Wealstun was one prison where characters were plentiful. In one corner of my dormitory was 'Porn King', who was inside for running an illicit sex shop in Leeds. There was Eddie, who ran a high class, escort agency in Newcastle and while he was serving his time, his wife took care of business. Another Teesside lad sharing my dormitory was John Scarth who used to get to go out on home visits. It was difficult for him and others like him who went on these visits because coming back to prison after enjoying a short spell outside, was a wrench. John was the only ex-fellow prisoner that I stayed in touch with after I was released, and 14 years on, we were still reminiscing. Sadly, John died recently but I will always remember the many laughs we had about our memories of Wealstun. He idolised our friend, Brian, and loved to talk about our days in there. We had a lot of laughs which may sound odd when talking about a prison. John was one of those prisoners who could do his time and somehow, never have a bad word for anyone, or upset anyone. He was one of the easiest going fellow prisoners I ever spent time with. He wasn't just a fellow prisoner and a cellmate, he was also a good friend who will be sadly missed by many people.

There was always something happening at Wealstun. One day we had to stop work and queue for hours to get inoculated for tuberculosis. After one of the foreign prisoners brought the disease into the prison, no one was allowed on or off the camp that day, the whole day was taken up just queuing.

That Christmas, I was asked to help with an event the prison was holding for local under-privileged children. It was held in the visiting room. Three of the lads wore Teletubby outfits while the kitchen lads put together a nice spread. It was my job to write everyone's names on sticky labels. When the kids arrived at the prison, they lit the place up. Mrs Tasker and several prison staff were there too. I recall asking Mrs Tasker if it was alright for me to write her first name, Stacey on her sticky label just in case she thought it disrespectful. She joined in with everything, even sitting on the floor unwrapping presents with the children. The kids had a great time playing games. They were all given toys and as they left for the night, we handed them story books and bags of sweets. It was times like this that really humbled me. We were connected with people whose lives were far worse than we thought ours to be.

One day I telephoned one of my mates, Billy, who was Acklington with me. He said he had a friend who wanted to meet me. She was called Tina and came from Germany. I thought it would be nice to have a pen pal and someone to visit me, so we started corresponding. Things moved very fast and six weeks later she was making arrangements for our wedding. Why I went along with this, I will never know but in prison, people cling to whatever affection they can find from the outside world. Other prisoners talked about their wives and girlfriends. This made me envious as I wasn't able to join the conversation. They were so affectionate at visiting time, I wished I could have someone waiting for me on the outside. That's why I encouraged Tina's plans and didn't try to slow things down. Six weeks after meeting, we were married. It was all arranged through a few phone calls and community visits. My probation officer was very concerned about my decision to get married and tried to warn me of the difficulties it could cause. She asked why everything was happening so quickly. She was apprehensive having seen similar cases to mine. I was determined to go through with it. I liked the thought of having a wife and a home to go out to once I was released. It made me feel as though I had turned a corner.

For our wedding day, I made an application to the wing Governor for a special community visit pass. This would mean an extension of the time I could spend outside the prison if it was sanctioned. The wing Governor was a nice man and deeply religious. I was asked to go and see him in his office about my request. He showed me an old school photograph he displayed in his office of him as a boy with his classmates two of whom were Bobby and Jackie Charlton. He sanctioned six hours which Mrs Tasker later extended to nine.

Community visits brought with them a lot of worry. If a prisoner doesn't return to the prison on time, it counts as having absconded. This results in loss of privileges or even an arrest if they were very late. I saw this rule waived once when snow storms made it impossible for several prisoners to return on time.

On 16 November 1996, Tina and I were married at York Registry Office. My mother and Donald stayed over in York and my sister and brother in law came along; my two nieces, Suzy and Chrissie, were bridesmaids. Some of Tina's friends were witnesses. After the wedding, Tina and I went into York for a few drinks. Prisoners are not supposed to drink alcohol while on community visits but when I got back to the prison, they turned a blind eye. When arriving back at the prison, we had to enter through the closed side where the main reception was. When the screw unlocked the gate for me, he asked to see my ring. This made me happy, I thought I finally had what I wanted. It seemed strange as I turned around to wave to my new bride and see her waving back at me in her wedding dress. I stepped over the threshold and I was back in prison.

Over time, Tina stopped visiting as often and I became more paranoid and more depressed. The lads would wind me up feeding my paranoia, telling me that she had someone else. If nothing, this taught me to keep my private life private. One day, I stormed into someone's dormitory to teach him a lesson for taunting me. He wasn't there but his cellmate was. I waited while ranting to his cellmate. I eventually got bored waiting and eventually calmed down. I didn't confront him after that, but I suspect his cellmate gave him a warning as he never spoke to me again. After a while I was able to move to the 'billets' which were smaller rooms for two men. There was a long waiting list for these rooms, so to put their names down, prisoners had to have at least a two year sentence. My new pad mate, Frank, was serving life for murder. The room was dirty and neglected which made me depressed and added to my anxiety about my marriage. I requested to move and was given a new cell with Mike who was also serving life for murder. The wing Governor had warned him that I was depressed, but Mike wasn't worried about this. He didn't let anything get him down and we had a laugh. He had managed to acquire a large colour television from the screws' office. Mike worked in the kitchen at a golf course in Leeds as part of his resettlement. Every night he would bring both of us a beef or pork sandwich with onions and gravy wrapped in tin foil from work. One morning, Mike shook me awake, telling me over and over that Diane was dead. Diane was the name of Mike's wife. I tried to tell him how sorry I was for him, until he interrupted to tell me he meant Princess Diana.

We watched the news reports all day and the funeral service, six days later. I saw Mike fighting back tears as Elton John sang *Candle in the Wind.* It was unusual to see a prisoner express such emotion in the presence of fellow prisoners. Prison teaches you to to hide our feelings.

I didn't hide my emotions well while I was having my problems with Tina. My life was in tatters because Tina had stopped visiting and writing to me altogether. As time passed, I deteriorated and started to become erratic. I even had one or two confrontations with some of my fellow prisoners.

Week after week, I would change into my prison clothing, ready for the visits that never happened. We had to wear prison clothing for visits so we couldn't mingle with the visitors and walk out with them. The visitors would arrive at the main gate and then be escorted along the driveway leading to the visitors' centre. Visiting time was meant to be a family event, yet some would use visits to be more adventurous. One of our former cellmates called Mark, who was at the end of an eight year stretch, had conceived a child while in prison. As bizarre as it sounds, I knew that some managed to have sex with their partners while serving their sentences. When I was in Acklington, I couldn't help but notice certain activity between couples going on in the visiting room. They were discreet but I could see they were fornicating. I could see women straddling their partner's lap while using the men's shirt tails to hide their body parts. They had no regard for the other visitors, or indeed, children who were there. I know some of the other prisoners were fed up with this activity being ignored by the staff. I wonder how many children have been conceived in a prison visitor's room.

In Wealstun, when prisoners were expecting a visit, they would congregate just outside the billets where they could see the main doors of the visitor's centre. They would try to get a glimpse of their wives, children, girlfriends, parents and friends, so they could wave across to them. This was one time I would see prisoners happy and in high spirits, smiling and eager to see their loved ones. I would stand with them week after week for over six months hoping that Tina would be there. I continued to send her visiting orders in the hope that one day, she would turn up. She never did.

Of course in Wealstun, some prisoners were allowed regular home leave where they could spend about five days a month at home as part of their reintegration. Originally, those serving more than four years could get home leave. This stopped just before I was sentenced, and became only permitted for lifers. The only fixed termers that were allowed to continue with home leave were those who had been sentenced before the changes were brought in.

One Saturday morning, a screw came to my room and told me to report to the main gate as my name was listed for a community visit. I knew I had sent a community visiting order to Tina but I didn't know if she was able to make it or not. I was searched and then asked to sign a form. We all had to do this for community visits. We also had to take the forms with us in case we needed to prove who we were, should we get stranded, break down and needed to report to the police station. It was to prevent us breeching our curfew and becoming classed as absconded.

Excited at the prospect of seeing Tina again after so long, I walked through the gate, but I couldn't see her anywhere. I wandered around the prison car park but there was no one there. It then hit me that it had all been a terrible mistake. My heart sank, and so did my mood, It was the final straw which led to a complete emotional decline. I went back to the office where I received an apology from the screw who realised he'd made a mistake. It was little comfort to my rapidly sinking spirit. Of all the times to make a mistake, why was it at that moment when I was already at rock bottom?

My family met me the following weekend and took me home for a community visit to try and help me. My spirit was broken so I spent the day drinking around Eston and reminiscing around the place where I grew up as a teenager. While drunk, I called Tina but she was cold towards me. I knew then that we were finished. I returned to prison, drunk, upset, and depressed. I cried in my room, and Mike was concerned about me. I went over to the closed side and asked to be segregated. I knew one of the screws from the open side. As he let me through I told him that I didn't want parole. I was charged with being drunk and disorderly. But while in solitary, I was able to really gather my thoughts and reflect. I started to become strong again. There were no prisoners messing with my head and I started to see things clearly for the first time in months. I was given daily exercise, for an hour in a small enclosed yard. I couldn't see sky or scenery there. Outside my cell, there were a few pay phones where prisoners' calls were always recorded. All prisons can record telephone conversations, but it is done randomly, whereas, in segregation, all conversations are recorded.

Unlike the 1980's, we could have a mattress in our cells all the time, but this rule had only changed while I was in solitary during 1996. In those three days, Europe changed the law, so I no longer had to leave my mattress outside the cell during the day. I had a cardboard chair and desk, several sheets of writing paper and a pen.

Having so little was the best thing that could have happened to me. My thoughts became clearer than ever. I decided to continue my studies and divorce Tina. This positive decision lifted the weight from my shoulders. I also applied to be considered for parole. I had my university offer on condition that I passed my exams and had secured a place at Tynebridge Hostel in North Shields, should I be granted parole. The last thing I wanted to do now was mess it all up. I started to panic once I started divorce proceedings. I had to quickly find somewhere to live to be granted parole because the original plan was to move in with my new wife. When applying for parole, prisoners must have a stable address. Luckily, my friend Ben introduced me to the staff at Tynebridge Housing who were involved in the aftercare of offenders who needed re-housing. Two of their staff members came to visit me in prison and were able to offer me a place at their hostel. Although this was a great relief to me, I was worried that the parole board would see my recent behaviour as erratic. Getting married to someone I hardly knew and then divorcing her within a year could have been seen as very impulsive behaviour. I fully expected this to jeopardise my parole, especially as my probation officer had expressed concerns about me deciding to marry someone I hardly knew in the first place. The day after I had been segregated, I was taken to the Governor. While I was in solitary, I had written a letter, which was handed to her. Mrs Tasker read out the charges and gave me five days in solitary and added seven days to my sentence before sending me back to the open side. She was a fair Governor. She supported education and accepted my plea to return to the open side to sit my exams and return to the closed side. She allowed me to continue my sentence on the open side though. She was compassionate and she was one of many who helped me through my education.

I felt that introducing pay phones on the prison landings was a bad idea. The phone queues were endless. It had been known for men to spend their entire two hours association time queuing for the phone, then to find no one's at home. If someone was really unlucky, they would get to the front of the queue after hours of waiting just to discover that they'd been sold a faulty phone card. And sometimes your conversation was cut short because association time was over and the phones were disconnected.

When prisoners call their families, all kinds of emotions can take over. Suddenly, you are connected to your front living room of your own home. You can hear background noises, televisions, door bells, and voices, all of which can make a prisoner very paranoid. Suddenly, your blood pressure rises, your mind begins to race and before you know it, accusations and a heated exchange follows. You're accusing your partner of sleeping with the milkman, best mate, or anyone your imagination conjures up. Prisoners partners are just as much prisoners as their partners.

Many men think that because they are in prison and have their freedom restricted, that their partners must live the same way. Although it is wrong to expect this, I understood these emotions. One prisoner telephoned his wife one day. Another man answered who told him that she was with him now. He hanged himself later that night.

At times, I could hear men working themselves up and screaming down the phone completely losing control. I recognised all of these emotions as I had felt them with Tina. She had also been abusive towards my mother and Uncle Donald who went to stay with her once. She locked them in her house once and accused them of interfering in our relationship. That was the last straw for me, so in October 1997, I rang a solicitor in Leeds and started divorce proceedings. Once I'd made that decision to divorce Tina, I felt a massive sense of relief. From that day on, I've always removed anything that causes me stress, because I now know what a huge relief it can bring.

During this period, I learned the importance of opening up. I stopped bottling things up and regularly went to see the prison probation officer to talk things through. One day while I was sat talking to my probation officer, ironically a telephone call was put through from Tina. She asked if I'd been released from prison because someone had put a brick through one of her windows. Of course, I had an air tight alibi. I was still in prison. But I felt a huge sense of Karma.

In 1997, electronic tags were introduced and I remember one of the office orderlies telling us that hundreds had been delivered to the prison. There were a lot of rumours as to who would get them and be released early. Those who were in for violent offences had no chance, so I knew I wouldn't be tagged. When the time came to start the project, hundreds were released early into the community. Then not long after, it was revealed that they had wrongly released hundreds of prisoners. They now had to go and round them all up again and bring them back to prison.

I was progressing with my Open University work, however, I needed to word process my essays. I hadn't used a computer before, so needed to gain some basic skills. I went on a Computer Literacy and Information Technology (CLAIT) course and learned how to use a computer and word processing software. I was getting good results and every two weeks, someone from the Open University would come and see me from Leeds to go through my assignments and discuss things with me. I posted some UCAS (University & Colleges Admissions Service) forms to several universities, including Teesside and Northumbria, applying for a place to study criminology on my release. I started receiving letters making conditional offers which meant I had a place on condition I passed my OU exams. I sat my exams one sunny afternoon in the education block's kitchen with the education manager, Mr Woodrow invigilating me.

The kitchen, which was normally used for teaching prisoners cooking skills was situated next to the visitor's room. It was visiting time and I could hear activity outside as visitors started to turn up. It was only a few days earlier that I had returned from the punishment block, but now I was feeling good about my exam. My mind was clear and I had worked hard towards this exam so was feeling confident. The education staff had supported me all the way through my studies. Several weeks later, my exam results arrived. I'd passed. This meant I could take up my place at Northumbria University to study criminology and from then on my life started to change. In early February 1998, I was on the computer in class, when Mrs Topping came in and told me that the wing officer, Mr McKnight, wanted to see me. Parole answers had been coming in recently, so I knew it had to be my turn. I had been nagging the wing officer for weeks about my answer, so it was a relief for us both when it came through. Waiting for parole had been a nightmare. The process takes months. From start to finish it includes being interviewed by a parole board member, collecting references, writing a statement about why you feel you should get parole followed by a very lengthy wait. The biggest thing that was in my favour of course, was my offer of a place Northumbria University. I was able to use it as an example in my parole dossier and part of my resettlement plan. It was quite an ordeal planning my future from prison. I needed to convince the parole board that I was taking responsibility for my actions. This wasn't just for the offence that landed me in prison, but also for the trouble I got into while I was in prison. I told them it was a mistake marrying Tina. I explained that it was a bad choice to turn to alcohol to deal with my problems. I emphasised that I still intended on making huge changes to my life, but needed support. My worry was that they would consider me as a high risk to the public after having resorted to old behavioural patterns in a time of an emotional crisis. It is the triggers that concern the authorities. For example, when I had a problem, I turned to alcohol and when I turned to alcohol, my risk of offending was high. My plan worked though, and although the parole board never gave reasons why they granted me parole, I believe that my university place swayed it for me.

I entered Mr McKnight's office, and was asked to sit down. I was to be released on the 9th February 1998. I was elated. I went straight to the education block to tell everyone and asked if I could spend the rest of the afternoon calling my family and making arrangements for the 9th.

20. Epilogue

That was 18 years ago now, the same year most of my undergraduate students were born, and although my journey from that day until now hasn't been easy, my life continues to improve. The first half of my life has been traumatic but as I enter my early fifties, I have a new and hungry zest for life that I was never able to enjoy when I had no prospects or goals. They say today's 50s are yesterday's 30s and this is exactly the premise from where I'm now living my life. I was in my early 30s when I was sent to prison so at least from this perspective I am able to turn back the clock and start again.

I've recently taken on my first role as a full time criminology lecturer at the University of York and I am nearing the end of my PhD journey. There is barely a day goes by that I don't regret my actions as my conscience continually reminds me of them. The fact I am beginning my academic career at the age of 53 itself, is a constant reminder of the wasted years which could have been spent forging my career. I wish I had been stable enough to have started my career at a much younger age as many of my much younger colleagues have done.

There is the irony though where my past also has its advantages. I have life experiences to draw on in my teaching which I know the students love to hear. I continue to self-analyse and change too. Life experiences that have had a profound impact on one's sense of self is not something that just ends. It's a continual lifetime journey and along the way, I learn more about myself and others. I have learned to manage my impulsiveness and things that would have once aggravated me hardly faze me at all. I have mother nature to thank for this as growing older has brought with it maturity and inner contentment. Therefore while I may regret the many wasted years, aging has been good to me. I can't achieve everything I want to, but I know I can and still have much work to do for myself and for others.

I wish so much that I will one day succeed in my chosen career and fulfill my dreams of being a successful academic. I wish I could pass on my knowledge to young people and show them the consequences of a life a crime. I wish I could convince them to stay on the straight and narrow and avoid a lifetime of misery and suffering. I wish, I wish, I wish!